# THEORY OF CATALOGUING

# THEORY OF CATALOGUING

AN EXAMINATION GUIDEBOOK—SECOND EDITION REVISED

BY PATRICK QUIGG ALA

SUB-LIBRARIAN QUEEN'S UNIVERSITY BELFAST

ARCHON BOOKS & CLIVE BINGLEY LTD

COPYRIGHT © CLIVE BINGLEY LTD 1968
ALL RIGHTS RESERVED
FIRST PUBLISHED 1966 BY CLIVE BINGLEY LTD
SECOND EDITION REVISED AND PUBLISHED 1968
THIS EDITION PUBLISHED IN THE UNITED STATES 1968
BY ARCHON BOOKS 60 CONNOLLY PARKWAY
HAMDEN CONNECTICUT 06514
PRINTED IN GREAT BRITAIN
208 00859 4

# CONTENTS

INTRODUCTION: *page* 7

CHAPTER ONE: PURPOSES OF CATALOGUING: *page* 9

CHAPTER TWO: HISTORY: *page* 14

CHAPTER THREE: DEVELOPMENT OF THE CODES: *page* 21

CHAPTER FOUR: COMPARISONS BETWEEN THE CODES: *page* 38

CHAPTER FIVE: PROBLEMS OF SPECIAL MATERIALS: *page* 50

CHAPTER SIX: INNER FORMS OF CATALOGUES: *page* 63

CHAPTER SEVEN: PHYSICAL FORMS OF CATALOGUES: *page* 74

CHAPTER EIGHT: CATALOGUING PROCESSES AND POLICIES: *page* 79

CHAPTER NINE: CATALOGUING AND INFORMATION RETRIEVAL METHODS: *page* 97

INDEXES: *page* 111

# INTRODUCTION

THE content of each chapter, and the sequence of chapters, have been related as closely as possible to the sectional headings in the UK Library Association syllabus, although it might be noted that chapter eight covers topics which, while not explicitly named in the syllabus, have emerged in the examination papers. In view of many developments in the application of computers to cataloguing, it seemed desirable to include a section on the computer and the catalogue, which has been located in chapter nine following discussion on information retrieval methods and mechanisms.

The text of the second edition has been revised to take into account the Anglo American Cataloguing Rules, 1967 (frequently designated in the text by the abbreviation AACR), chapters three, four and five being particularly extended. Several other matters dealt with in the first edition, *eg* the Shared Cataloguing Programme, Project MARC at LC (and now at BNB), developments in computer cataloguing etc, have been updated and rewritten Many of the references cited in the text and in the readings have been revised in the light of recently published articles and books.

Basic texts for the subject will be evident from the readings cited at the end of each chapter, in which the recurrence of citations to the books by Coates, Jolley, Mann, Needham and Sharp indicate their value for this purpose. These readings are, of course, additional to those cited throughout the text.

The following abbreviations have been used in many places in the text: AA, Anglo-American code (1908); ALA, American Library Association; ALA 3 (etc), American Library Association *Cataloguing rules for author and title entries* (1949) rule 3 (etc); BM, British Museum; BM 18 (etc), *British Museum rules* rule 18 (etc); BNB, *British national bibliography*; DC, Dewey's decimal classification; ICCP, International Conference on Cataloguing Principles, Paris, 1961; IFLA, International Federation of Library Associations; LC, Library of Congress; RDC, *Rules for descriptive cataloguing in the Library of Congress;* UDC Universal decimal classification.

PATRICK QUIGG

# CHAPTER ONE
# PURPOSES OF CATALOGUING

**B**OOKS and documents in a collection can be physically arranged consistently and usefully by one factor only, usually subject, or perhaps, as in the case of fiction, author. On the catalogue, therefore, falls the purpose of providing, by means of a multiple sequence of entries, access to the collection through most of the other principal channels by which the reader may seek documents. The full library catalogue should be an instrument equipped to deal with the several channels of enquiry, and of essential importance to the successful identification and retrieval of books and documents, no matter what pattern of arrangement is applied to the material on the shelves.

Cutter defined the purpose of the catalogue in his *Rules* thus:

1 To enable a person to find a book of which either: *a*) the author is known, *b*) the title is known, *c*) the subject is known.

2 To show what the library has: *d*) by a given author, *e*) on a given subject, *f*) in a given kind of literature.

3 To assist in the choice of a book: *g*) as to its edition (bibliographically), *h*) as to its character (literary or topical).

Cutter's objectives *a*) and *c*) are indisputable. Objective *b*), while usually interpreted, in the case of works with personal authors, to cover only significant or striking titles, also includes all those documents for which the title entry would be the principal one, *eg* periodicals.

Objective *d*) encounters the difficulty of such traditional problems as authors writing under different pseudonyms, successive changes of name, etc. These problems have generated many rules in many codes.

Objective *e*) might nowadays be amplified to cover not only the 'given subject', but also 'related subjects', although Cutter's (and the dictionary catalogue's) focus on specificity is perhaps reflected here.

Objective *f*) covered by 'form entries' is usually approached on a selective basis, since the amount of material that can be entered under a form heading such as DICTIONARIES can be vast.

Objective *g*) is covered by the descriptive cataloguing of the work and there is much evidence of heart searching by cataloguers throughout the years about the desired fullness of description in relation to the purposes of cataloguing.

Objective *h*), a matter of notes and annotation, can nowadays rarely be achieved in a large catalogue except perhaps, as in the case of *f*), on a selective basis.

Nevertheless, Cutter's examination of the aims and purposes of cataloguing remains substantially valid, and later statements are most usually re-statements of them.

The 1961 International Conference on cataloguing principles enumerated the author/title catalogue function as to show: 1 whether the library contains a particular book specified by *a*) its author and title; *or b*) if the author is not named in the book, its title alone; *or c*) in the absence of author and title, a suitable substitute for the title, and 2 which works by a particular author and which editions of a particular work are in the library. Mary Piggott, reporting the Conference findings, says: 'Thus Cutter's objectives, in so far as they relate to author entry, remain unchanged, and so do his means of main entry, added entries or references under author and title as the case may require' (*Assistant librarian* 55 (11), 1962 212).

Shera and Egan (page 9 of *The classified catalog* cited below) more briefly state the objectives: 'The conclusion from both experience and analysis seems inescapable that there are two basic functions of the catalog that are of outstanding importance: 1 accurate and speedy determination of whether or not an item known by author or title is in the collection, and, if so, of where it may be found; and 2 what materials the library contains upon a given subject and where they may be found.'

This statement suggests a lessening of the bibliographical-identification function (objective *g*), which is increasingly being shouldered by 'published bibliographic services'.

Most of the discussion on catalogue function will nevertheless be found to be centred on debating, evaluating and perhaps modifying one or more of the objectives stated by Cutter.

Some of the questions that have to be asked concern:
1 The possible 'inventory' function of the catalogue which, while probably the original function, is now almost obsolete in the light of the shelf-list.

2 The conflict between the catalogue as an uncomplicated 'finding list' for the location of specific books, and the catalogue as a bibliographical instrument assembling 'groups' of books under uniform headings. Paul Dunkin's remarks are worth reading on this point, in his explanatory commentary which runs as parallel text in S Lubetsky *Code of cataloguing rules: an unfinished draft* (ALA 1960 pages 9 to 15).

3 Following upon this, the possible relation of the catalogue function to that of the general bibliographical apparatus.

4 The conflict that may exist between the catalogue functioning as a working tool for the professional staff and as an instrument available to the general reader.

Question 2, finding list versus bibliographical instrument or reference tool, provides, perhaps, the most vexing area of enquiry in the light of constantly increasing cataloguing costs. There is some evidence that the 'finding list function' has gained a slight advantage in the debate. The University of Oxford *Report of the Committee on University Libraries* (Oxford, 1966), otherwise known as the *Shackleton report*, which examines the situation regarding libraries and catalogues in Oxford impressively, and at length, states in measured terms (Par 320), '... the question should be asked, is a library catalogue to be regarded as a series of irreproachable bibliographical documents, or as a means of finding books? We take, without hesitation, the second view.' In the *Statement of principles adopted by the ICCP, Annotated edition with commentary and examples* by A H Chaplin and Dorothy Anderson (IFLA Secretariat, 1966) it is noted (page 4) that the function of collocating works by a particular author, and identifying editors ' was considered by some of the delegates to the conference to be less important' than the finding list function. However, the commentary states that even if the second function were omitted, ' many of the principles designed to provide for it would still be needed: the user of the catalogue will not always be able to specify a book by the particular form of its author's name, or the particular title, which occurs in the edition actually present in the library'. The new *Anglo-American cataloguing rules, 1967* with their emphasis on what might be called the 'user-oriented' heading, the form of name by which the author, personal or corporate, is *commonly* identified, might be claimed to this extent to be shaped towards acceptance of the fact that the catalogue should function firstly as a finding list.

Again, the continuing and accelerating movement towards the automation of library processes, has brought a fresh approach to bear on the question of catalogue function. The required careful analysis of those operations involved in computerisation tends to produce a situation in which such analysis cannot be confined merely to the operations themselves, but must extend to their purposes and to their ends. In the automated library, the catalogue lies at the very heart of the system, and consequently its form, function and purpose is being subjected continually to constant re-examination in innumerable library automation conferences, institutes, workshops, and working parties. Nothing very striking has so far emerged and there is often the feeling that old problems are being re-stated in a new guise. However, Ritvars Bregzis ' The Bibliographic Information Network: some suggestions for a different view of the library catalogue ' chapter nine, pages 128-142 in *The Brasenose conference on the automation of libraries* argues that the computer can produce a 'reactive catalogue', that it can generate from a common bibliographical data store, a *system* of catalogues that are all mutually compatible and fully mechanised with transference from one to the other being easily effected. One generated catalogue might serve the finding list function ('the bibliographic data form orientation'), another might be generated, whenever required, to serve the requirements of ' bibliographic data correlation' *ie* providing a catalogue serving as a bibliographical tool assembling literary units. If such a development is achievable (and economically viable) then the conflict of purpose and function in this area of the library catalogue may be finally resolved.

READINGS

E J Coates *Subject catalogues: headings and structure* (London, Library Association 1960) chapter three ' The two-fold objective '.
L Jolley *The principles of cataloguing* (London, Crosby Lockwood 1961) chapter one ' The function of the catalogue '.
M Mann *Introduction to cataloguing and the classification of books* (Chicago, ALA, second edition 1943) chapter one ' The purpose and scope of cataloguing '.
R K Olding, editor *Readings in library cataloguing* (London,

Crosby Lockwood 1966) Lubetzky's statement of Objectives and Implications page 249, and the editor's prefatory note to this reading, pages 243-244.

J H Shera and M E Egan *The classified catalogue: basic principles and practice* (Chicago, ALA 1956) chapter one ' The nature and function of the catalog '.

# CHAPTER TWO: HISTORY

THE history of cataloguing can be considered from several aspects, notable contributions made by librarians, the influence wielded by institutions, societies and conferences, the development of catalogues of various kinds, and of codes of rules and practice. The latter subject, cataloguing codes, will be dealt with in chapter three, while specific forms of catalogues will be referred to where appropriate throughout the text.

Dorothy M Norris, in her *History of cataloguing and cataloguing methods 1100-1850* (London, Grafton 1939) has dealt with the history of the early period. She includes an 'introductory survey of ancient times' recognising that the catalogues fall naturally into four groups:

1 Ancient catalogues to AD 1100, 'Scanty material, difficult to find, frequently contradictory';

2 Medieval monastic catalogues 1100-1400, of which she says 'it would be impossible to describe more than a few';

3 Collegiate (or academic) catalogues 1400-1700 (three chapters, including one on the Bodleian Library catalogues);

4 Catalogues from 1700 onwards, including a chapter on the British Museum catalogues.

Norris ends her study at that period, the middle of the nineteenth century, when it might be said modern cataloguing practice really had its beginnings. This was essentially the age when individual librarians made major contributions.

Sir Anthony Panizzi (1797-1879), Keeper of Printed Books at the British Museum in 1837, later Principal Librarian (1856), was the central figure in the 'battle of the rules' controversy which raged around the deficiency and slowness of production of the British Museum catalogues. With his associates (including J Winter Jones and Edward Edwards) he formulated the first version of the famous 91 rules which were accepted in 1839 and published in 1841. Panizzi's code embodied many of the cataloguing principles upon which other subsequent codes were drawn up and it was widely acclaimed throughout the library world. A full account will be found in chapter ten of Norris' book. The fascinating dialogue between Panizzi and the 'Commissioners appointed to inquire' is reproduced as the first reading, pages 5-29 in R K Olding *Readings in library cataloguing* (cited below).

Charles C Jewett (1816-1868), when librarian of Brown University USA, published an author catalogue to which was appended an alphabetical 'topical index' in 1843. Later, in 1852, as librarian of the Smithsonian Institution, he published a report *On the construction of catalogues of libraries*, in which he set forth the first American rules for author entry and suggested an alphabetical list of subjects as supplementary to the 'general' catalogue. Julia Pettee in her book (cited below) names Jewett, not Cutter, as 'father of our modern library methods' and points to his influence as far afield as the Liverpool catalogue of 1872.

Andrea Crestadoro (1808-79) was a reader in the British Museum at the time when there was still great unhappiness about the progress of the cataloguing. In 1856 he issued a pamphlet *The art of making catalogues of libraries* advocating detailed main entries, each entry beginning with the author's name. The main entries needed 'no particular arrangement', however, but were to be supplemented by an index of names and subjects, essentially alphabetical in arrangement, connected by cross references. He later became the third city librarian of Manchester where, although the 1864 reference catalogue appeared with main entries alphabetically arranged, the supplementary volumes 1864-79 were arranged according to his theory.

Charles A Cutter (1837-1903), when making the *Catalogue of the library of the Boston Athenaeum* (five volumes 1874-82), not only worked out his systematic dictionary plan therein, but in 1876 published his *Rules for a printed dictionary catalogue*. His rules for author/title entries not only had an obvious influence on the AA code and on subsequent American practice, but those for subject headings, some half dozen pages, have formed the basis of subject heading practice until the present day.

These four librarians typify the achievement of individuals in the nineteenth century formative era of modern cataloguing. In the middle of the 1870's, however, the Library Associations of the UK and the USA were formed, and corporate agreements in the form of codes of rules (see chapter three) and the examples and practice demonstrated by the developing catalogues of the large libraries (particularly when their catalogues were published) became more influential than individual voices.

The decision of the Library of Congress, upon reorganisation in the period 1899-1901, to choose the dictionary catalogue and to print its cards, so making them available to other libraries, has made it a dominant influence on US cataloguing practice ever since, as evidenced by the authority of such publications as the *List of subject headings and Rules for descriptive cataloguing*. (The latter now having provided the basis for the Rules for Description in the *Anglo-American Cataloguing Rules*, 1967.)

The British Museum Library, whose catalogue entries were not ever available in the same way, did not achieve, or indeed seek, a similar role. However, since the 1950's with the BNB cataloguing the books received by copyright deposit in the British Museum and providing (since 1956) printed cards for them, there is every indication of the emergence of a similar pattern.

Indeed, in the spate of conferences and codes during the twentieth century, only one name has seemed to emerge to anything like the prominence of the earlier cataloguing theorists. Seymour Lubetzky, consultant on bibliographic and cataloguing policy in the Library of Congress, was invited by the ALA to prepare a study of the much-criticised 1949 ALA rules. His *Cataloguing rules and principles* (Washington, Library of Congress 1953) criticised the code on the grounds of having too numerous rules, with overlapping, duplication, and inconsistency, and proposed that a revised code should be based more upon general principles, rather than consist of attempted enumeration of all possible difficulties and problems. His critique provided a penetrating analysis of the theory and practice of cataloguing, against which the codification of catalogue rules and the making of catalogues had to be re-examined.

Much valuable knowledge of the history of catalogues and cataloguing can be gained by study of the actual catalogues in their various forms. Below is a list of printed catalogues (many of the more recently published being available in larger libraries), which is arranged chronologically in the various categories of 'inner form' of the catalogue. Available examples from these lists should serve to illustrate not only the general history of cataloguing, but also the chapter on inner forms of catalogues.

## AUTHOR CATALOGUES

The *British Museum catalogues* provide a conspectus of catalogue history ranging from the two volume catalogue of 1787, the seven volume catalogue of 1813-19, and the catalogues of 1881-1905 (ninety-five volumes with fifteen supplementary volumes). Publication of the catalogue begun in 1931, was suspended in 1954 after fifty-one volumes to letters DEZW had been published. In great contrast to its ill-fated predecessor, the photo-lithographic publication of the *General catalogue of printed books* was signally successful, the entire production being achieved in the space of six years. Covering holdings up to 1955, it commenced publication in 1959 and was completed in October 1966 with a total of 263 volumes containing over four million entries. Supplementary volumes listing additions for the years 1963 (five volumes), 1964 (seven volumes), 1965 (six volumes) have been published, while publication of a cumulated ten-year supplement for the years 1956-1965 in approximately fifty volumes containing 700,000 entries commenced in 1968. Peter Brown ' GK 3 the end of an era ' *Catalogue & index* 1 (5) Jan 1967 pages 1 and 12, briefly recounts the history of the publication of the several British Museum Catalogues over the years, concluding by predicting that, with the advent of automation, the era of the highly successful photo-lithography process nevertheless will prove to be short.

The *Catalogue of the London Library* was first issued in 1847. The latest edition of the main catalogue (two volumes 1913-14, with supplementary volumes published in 1920, 1929 and 1953) follows the pattern designed by Sir Charles H Wright. There are separately published subject indexes (four volumes published at intervals 1909-1955). The *John Rylands Library Manchester catalogue of printed books* (three volumes 1899) and the *Edinburgh University Library catalogue of printed books* (three volumes 1918-1923) are representative of their period.

Contrasting examples of the production of author catalogues of great national libraries can be found in 1 the *Catalogue général des livres imprimés* of the Bibliothèque Nationale, which published volume 1 in 1897 and in 1966 was still on letter ' T ', each volume therefore representing the acquisitions up to the date of printing of the volume; and 2 *Library of Congress catalog: books: authors* which by photolithography reproduced its printed card entries in page form in 167 volumes covering its holdings up to

17

1942. Two twenty-four volume supplements brought it up to 1952, and it is continued by the *National union catalog* (which includes author entries contributed by other US research libraries) appearing at monthly, quarterly, annual and five yearly cumulations.

Publications of the largest book catalogue ever, the *National union catalog, pre-1956 imprints*, has been undertaken by the Library of Congress. The catalogue will appear in an estimated 610 volumes published over ten years, and contain some sixteen million entries covering the location of ten million titles in 700 North American libraries. The firm which produced the British Museum *General catalogue* were awarded the contract and have issued a volume describing the vast undertaking: *Prospectus for the national union catalog, pre-1956 imprints* (London, Mansell, 1967).

CLASSIFIED CATALOGUES

Some early examples of the classified catalogue include: *Catalogue of the Signet Library Edinburgh* issued by George Sandy in 1827; *Royal Institution Library catalogue* ' methodically ' arranged with an author index, issued by William Harris in 1809; *Cambridge University, Queen's College Library catalogue* ' methodically ' arranged, issued by Thomas Hartwell Horne in 1827.

*The Literary and Philosophical Society of Newcastle-upon-Tyne Library catalogue* of 1903 was classified by DC and had author and subject indexes. *Glasgow Public Libraries union catalogue of additions* (six volumes for the period 1929-1955), and *Westminster Public Libraries classified catalogue of non-fiction additions 1952-* are good examples of contemporary printed classified catalogues.

US examples of classified catalogues (printed by photo-reproduction of the existing card catalogues) are *American Geographical Society research catalogue* begun in 1923, published 1962; and *Engineering Societies Library, New York classed subject catalog* begun in 1913 using UDC, published in 1963.

DICTIONARY CATALOGUES

Early examples are: *Birmingham Reference Library catalogue* issued 1869 by J D Mullins on the ' title-a-line ' basis; *Liverpool Reference Library catalogue* (1872); Cutter's five volume *Boston*

*Athenaeum Library catalogue* (1874-82); *Peabody Institute, Baltimore library catalogue* (thirteen volumes 1883-1905) with many analytical entries; *Index-catalogue of the library of US Surgeon-General's office* begun in 1880 by John Shaw Billings, perhaps the most splendid early example of dictionary cataloguing combined with periodical and analytical indexing (continued since 1950 as *National Library of Medicine catalog*).

*Liverpool Public Libraries catalogues of non-fiction added* (four volumes 1925 to 1959); and *Bristol Public Libraries annual catalogues of additions* provide two examples of current dictionary catalogues. Bristol have also recently issued (1962) a five volume dictionary catalogue of non-fiction published prior to 1955.

US examples of dictionary catalogues (photo-reproduced from card catalogues) are *Metropolitan Museum of Art, New York catalog* (twenty five volumes Boston, G K Hall 1960) and *Columbia University School of Library Service dictionary catalog* (six volumes Boston, G K Hall 1962). Any available examples of G K Hall reproductions can be studied with great profit since they reproduce so directly the original catalogue entries.

SUBJECT CATALOGUES

The *Subject index of modern works added to the library of the British Museum* covers the period from 1881 to 1960, although a gap presently exists for the years 1951 to 1955. The six volumes for 1956 to 1960, produced in a larger format, were published out of sequence because 'of a different method of preparing copy'. The BM *Subject index* is an alphabetical subject catalogue with somewhat erratic variations in headings and subdivisions between the quinquennial issues from 1902.

*London Library subject index* (1909 with three supplementary volumes 1920, 1929, 1953). A detailed alphabetical subject catalogue with certain eccentricities *eg* singular noun often (but not always) preferred in subject headings.

*Library of Congress catalog: books: subjects* (1950-1954 twenty volumes; 1955-1959 twenty two volumes). Monthly issues, quarterly, annual and quinquennial cumulation. Begun as complement to author catalogue and interesting as an example of Congress subject headings in use.

The above three subject catalogues are respectively characterised as 'a conscientious civil servant' (BM); 'a competent British lady'

(London Library); 'an organization man caught in a tremendous machine' (LC) in Archer Tayler *General subject-indexes since 1548* (Philadelphia, University of Philadelphia Press, 1966) chapter 7 pages 298-304. The book is concerned with subject bibliographies more than subject catalogues of libraries, but the above section, which deals particularly with the history of the compilation of the London Library Subject-index is worth consultation.

READINGS

J Metcalfe *Subject classifying and indexing of libraries and literature* (Sydney, Angus and Robertson 1959) chapter three 'Catalogues and indexes from past to present'.

R K Olding *Readings in library cataloguing* (London, Crosby Lockwood, 1966). The reading on Panizzi has been cited above. The editor's introductory notes and the readings from other writers, particularly Cutter, Osborn and Lubetsky should be noted.

J Pettee *Subject headings: history and theory of the alphabetical approach to books* (New York, Wilson 1946) chapter two 'History of the dictionary catalogue', deals particularly with US catalogues.

H A Sharp *Cataloguing: a textbook for use in libraries* (London, Grafton fourth edition 1948) chapter twenty-five 'History of catalogues'.

R F Strout 'The development of the catalog and cataloguing codes' *Library quarterly* 25 (4) October 1956 254-275. A concise and readable account of catalogue history.

# CHAPTER THREE
# DEVELOPMENT OF THE CODES

1841 BRITISH MUSEUM RULES: *Rules for compiling the catalogue of printed books, maps and music in the British Museum* (London, British Museum revised edition 1936).

When originally published in 1841 there were 91 rules. The current edition has 41 rules with additional unnumbered rules in the last two chapters for maps and music. The code was designed for an alphabetical catalogue arranged primarily under authors' names in which only one ' main ' entry would carry fairly full bibliographical details with shorter ' added' entries often being preferred to simple cross-references.

Its importance lies not only in the fact of its continuing application to the catalogue of a great national library, but also in its primacy *ie* it was the ' founding code ', being the first systematic code of rules drawn up to guide the compiler of an author catalogue. All later codes derived to some extent from it. Again it had immediate influence on the rules of other large libraries such as the Bodleian and Cambridge University and less directly perhaps, but just as importantly, upon the decisions of subsequent code committees.

The features that emerge in contrast to subsequent codes relate principally to works that tend to lack personal names in their authorship. The broad philosophy underlying this matter would appear to be towards avoiding direct title entry except as a last resort, by extracting any element from the title of the work that might be used as a heading, *eg* the sixth and *last* alternative for entry of anonymous work is under first word of title not an article (BM 18f). The concept of ' corporate authorship ' first emerged in BM. Another singular feature is the kind of classified element introduced by the use of such form headings for main entries as ' dictionaries, encyclopaedias, directories ' etc. Although policy seems to tend towards their gradual removal (academies and congresses have already been dispersed in the current catalogue) such a heading as 'periodical publications' is still the main entry heading, subdivided by place, for all periodicals not issued by a society or institution.

A most readable evaluative account of BM rules by A H Chaplin, 'Reconsideration of the BM rules—2', will be found in *Cataloguing principles and practice* edited by M Piggott (London, LA 1954) pages 37-49. The preceding related chapter bearing the same title (chapter three, pages 26-36) by F C Francis deals concisely with the history and origins of the code (including the 'acrimonious controversy').

1876 CUTTER'S RULES: *Rules for a dictionary catalog* by Charles A Cutter (Washington Government Printing Office, fourth edition 1904).

The first edition (1876) had 205 rules, which were tested by application to the catalogue of the Boston Athenaeum Library, which Cutter compiled. The fourth edition, published in the year after his death, has 369 rules, covering not only rules for author/title entry and description, but also form entry, alphabetical subject entry and the filing of entries. It was and is the most complete set of rules ever produced by an individual, and provided the first extensive codification of cataloguing practice in the form of copious notes on many matters of difficulty, frequently enunciating principles that continue to be studied to the present day.

Its importance lies not only in this latter area but on the influence Cutter's pragmatic approach has had upon American practice, particularly evident in the US alternative rules in the AA code. Cutter emphasised in many ways that the 'convenience of the user should be preferred to the ease of the cataloguer', and recommendations to use the 'best known' form of author's name and to follow 'customary use of the names of subjects' reflect this approach. By enunciating the principle of specific subject entry and connective referencing he laid the foundations for all subsequent dictionary catalogue practice. In the principle that the catalogue should not only facilitate the finding of a given book but should also fulfil the other object of showing what the library has under a given author, he reinforced the contention that the catalogue should assemble literary units.

Other features of the code include: rules for corporate authorship more developed and numerous than BM with valuable discussion on the difficulties; provision for short, medium and full cataloguing to suit different styles of catalogues recognised; double entry recommended quite often when no one alternative is completely acceptable. A list of objectives is given at the beginning of the code, followed by comprehensive list of definitions. Rules arranged—ENTRY (where to enter) 1 author catalog 2 title catalog 3 subject catalog 4 form catalog. STYLE (how to enter) covering description and filing arrangement. Rules for cataloguing special materials (MSS, music, maps etc) by other compilers are included at the end of the work.

Concise accounts of Cutter's *Rules* will be found in: D M Norris *A primer of cataloguing* (London, AAL 1952) pages 103-106, and C D Needham *Organizing knowledge in libraries* (London, Deutsch 1964) pages 32-33.

1899 THE PRUSSIAN INSTRUCTIONS: *Instruktionen für die alphabetischen Kataloge der preussischen Bibliotheken.* 1899. *2 Ausgabe.* 1908 (Berlin, 1915).

*The Prussian instructions; rules for the alphabetical catalogues of the Prussian libraries* translated from the second edition by Andrew Osborn (Ann Arbor, 1938).

*Regeln für die alphabetische Katalogisierung in wissenschaftlichen Bibliotheken* (Leipzig, 1959).

In 1886, Professor K Dziatzko published his *Instruktionen für die ordnung der Titel im alphabetischen Zettelkatalog der Königlichen und Universitäts-Bibliothek zu Breslau.* This earlier German code formed the basis for the *Prussian instructions* (and was also the framework for K A Linderfelt's *Eclectic card catalogue rules,* 1890, the pioneer work in comparing cataloguing rules, which compared Dziatzko's rules with those of BM, Cutter and other authorities). The *Prussian instructions* were applied with great success to the German *Union catalogue* produced by the Prussian State Library—the *Deutscher Gesamtkatalog*—which drew many libraries in Germany and Austria into conformity with the rules, the philosophy being agreement on essentials, freedom on details. Co-operative cataloguing among German libraries in the earlier part of this century thus became a working reality when it was still little practised elsewhere.

The sections of the rules include: the entry of titles in alphabetical card catalogues; arrangement of titles; arrangement under authors' names; arrangement under real titles; alphabetical arrangement of authors' names and real titles. Appendices include: transliteration scheme; description of incunabula; rules for use of capital letters.

Essential differences to Anglo-American practice are: 1 the non-acceptance of the principle of corporate authorship, entry being made under title and 2 the *grammatical* arrangement of title entries, as compared to Anglo-American practice of natural word order. Andrew Osborn in his article ' Cataloguing and cataloguing codes in other countries today' *Library quarterly* 25 (4) October 1956 276-285 discusses the code at some length and states 'Three features stand out . . . 1 it is not a theoretical utterance but consists of carefully thought out rules . . . based on practical experience; 2 wording throughout is clear and unambiguous, all terms being defined; 3 the grasp of essentials displayed by its framers is truly noteworthy'.

A brief account of the *Prussian instructions* can be found in C G Viswanathan *Cataloguing theory and practice* (third edition London, Asia Publishing House 1965). A new German code, influenced by the acceptance of the Paris Principles is in course of preparation and a first instalment, a set of rules for the entry of corporate authors, has been produced by the Verein Deutscher Bibliothekare *Regeln für die alphabetische Katalogisierung, Teilenwurf, 1965*.

1908 AA CODE: *Cataloguing rules: author and title entries compiled by committees of the Library Association and the American Library Association* (1908).

Variously known as the *Joint code,* the *Anglo-American code,* the AA *Code.* In 1904, the two associations, having previously produced independent codes and being engaged in revising them agreed to co-operate in the production of a joint code which would bring uniformity into the cataloguing practice of the English-speaking countries. Melvil Dewey, a member of the US committee, had written a letter to the LA committee making this proposal in 1900, and the idea was taken up. Four years of deliberation and consultation produced the 1908 *Code* which is still the basic code for British practice to-day.

The 174 rules relate to the entry, heading and descriptive cataloguing of works for an author and title catalogue ' guided chiefly by the requirements of larger libraries of a scholarly character'. The prefaces acknowledge, and the notes throughout the text indicate, the influence of Cutter, Linderfelt's eclectic rules, Dziatzko and the *Prussian instructions,* and the BM and LC *Rules.*

Its importance lies in the fact of its being the first international cataloguing code, in the extent of its rapid and widespread adoption and use by all kinds and sizes of libraries in the two countries since its introduction, and in its continued use in Britain (although throughout the fifty-odd years of its use here there has been an ever-growing tendency towards modification and amplification, accelerated by the 1941 and 1949 ALA codes).

How long it will continue to exist in many and various annotated versions in British libraries in view of the publication of the *Anglo-American Cataloguing Rules, 1967* is a matter for some speculation.

The arrangement was an improvement in preceding codes. The ' Entry and heading section ' (AA 1-135) is divided into personal authors, corporate authors, title entries; the remaining rules (AA 136-174) cover description. Much importance has been attached to the occasions when the two committees failed to agree, but this happened with just eight rules out of 174 and centred principally upon the British (and BM tradition) of preferring the earliest of variant names and titles, while US (and Cutter's) practice tended towards the latest or ' best known '. The sample entries illustrating rules have always been the source of much criticism in that many are in German and Latin. The section on corporate authorship, with its undefined distinction and differential treatment of institutions (under place) and societies (under name), has provided grounds for much conflict throughout the years. A list of definitions of terms precedes the rules, but there is nowhere any statement of principles or purpose, nowadays considered so important.

A good critical assessment of the AA *Code* is to be found in C D Needham *Organizing knowledge in libraries* (London, Deutsch 1964) pages 33-36. E L J Smith's article 'Anglo-American *Code*' in Landau *Encyclopaedia of librarianship* (third edition London, Bowes 1966) is a concise reading on its origin and development.

1931 VATICAN CODE: Biblioteca Apostolica Vaticana: *Norme per il catalogo degli stampati. Terza edizione* (Citta del Vaticano 1949).

*Vatican Library*: *rules for the catalog of printed books* translated from the second Italian edition . . . edited by Wyllis E Wright (Chicago, ALA 1948).

The reorganization of the rich resources of the Vatican Library was begun in the 1920's. The Carnegie Endowment for International peace subsidised and collaborated in the project, sending, in 1928, four eminent American librarians, Martel, Hanson, Bishop, Randall, who were assisted by American-trained Vatican librarians, to revise the cataloguing practice of the library. The choice of the dictionary form of catalogue and the subsequent provision of printed cards are evidence of the American influence, while a very valuable product of the Commission was the emergence of the new cataloguing rules.

The basis of the codification was the Italian cataloguing rules of 1911 with the addition of suitable elements of the AA *Code* to 'internationalize' the Italian rules. However, it was found necessary further to widen the scope of these rules and to provide guidance in the development of subject headings. John Ansteinsson, a Norwegian librarian who had studied in the US, again re-worked the *Rules* after the departure of the other members of the Commission and the resulting code was published by the Vatican in 1931.

The first edition, a work of about 400 pages, contained some 500 rules covering the whole field of author/title entry, description, subject entry and filing. It was quickly accepted by cataloguers in many countries as the best and most complete code then in existence. An expanded second edition was published in 1939. During the thirties and forties the Vatican code was frequently cited as 'the best statement of American cataloguing practice', 'the most complete code for subject heading work' etc, although the English translation was not available until 1948, by which time the ALA (1949) rules were about to appear.

It has been stated that while the author entry and descriptive cataloguing sections have been less useful and influential than they might have been if translated earlier, nevertheless part 3, 'Subject headings', is unequalled in any language in its treatment of the fundamental principles of subject entry, and is the most important treatment since Cutter. The subject headings section is divided into two major parts, the first dealing with general principles and form, and the second with application to special areas—history, language, literature, geographical subjects. The subject heading dilemma, first raised by Cutter, of place versus subject is treated, but the compilers submit that frequently only subjective judgement can be the basis of decision.

An informative review of the English translation of the second edition has been provided by J H Shera 'Vatican library: rules for the catalog of printed books' *Library quarterly* 18 (4) October 1948 299-302.

1949 ALA RULES: ALA *Cataloguing rules for author and title entries* (Chicago, American Library Association, second edition, 1949).

*Rules for descriptive cataloging in the Library of Congress* (Washington, Government Printing Office 1949).

These two codes conjointly took the place of the AA *Code* in US cataloguing practice. In the period preceding acceptance and in the period following, cataloguers continued to evince much discontent with the complexity and lack of principles in codification of rules.

Between 1936 and 1939 both Library Associations co-operated in preparation for a new joint code but the outbreak of war put an end to British participation. The ALA proceeded independently and produced their 'preliminary' second edition of the *Code* in 1941 in two parts 1 'entry and heading', 2 'description of book', in which the 174 rules of the AA *Code* had grown to 375. The 1941 version was widely assailed on the grounds of complexity, overelaboration and too extensive enumeration of cases, the most famous attack being that of A D Osborn 'The crisis in cataloguing' *Library quarterly* 11 (4) October 1941 393-411, also printed in *Library assistant* 35 (4) April 1942 54-62 and 35 (5) May 1942 69-75.

The article has been reprinted in R K Olding *Readings in Library cataloguing* (already cited in the preceding chapter). It is one of the classic statements in cataloguing theory and, certainly, one of the historical turning points in code development. Among other things, Osborn convincingly demolished the three schools of cataloguers which he described as the 'legalistic', 'perfectionist' and 'bibliographical' practitioners, and thus heralded the beginning of a new era in reappraisal of cataloguing codes and practices.

The ALA Division of Cataloguing and Classification undertook revision of part 1 in 1946 and produced the 1949 code which is limited to author and title entries, the LC *Rules for descriptive cataloguing* (1949) being accepted as a substitute for the abandoned part 2 of the 1941 version.

The ALA rules number 158, but with numerous sections and subsections to each rule, they occupy some 226 pages compared to the 61 pages of the AA *Code* rules. They are organised into four groups: 1 rules of entry and heading (35 rules, 81 pages); 2 personal authors: form of entry (35 rules, 42 pages); 3 corporate bodies as authors (79 rules, 91 pages); 4 geographic headings (7 rules, 5 pages). Two rules covering added entries and references complete the code. Appendices cover i) glossary ii) abbreviations in headings iii) rules of style iv) translation.

The 'introduction' states that the ALA *Rules* 'are intended to represent the best or the most general current practice in cataloguing . . . the rules are not few nor are they, in total, simple . . . exceptions or qualifications are made when too strict an application of a general rule would result in a heading not giving the most direct approach . . .'

While it may be said that the arrangement of the rules is better than AA, that it lists more forms of literature and that the examples of the rules are better and more plentiful, yet to many of its critics it represented the continuance of the 'legalistic' approach criticised years before by Osborn.

'The codes became a maze of legalistic bypaths . . . an infinite variety of intricate exceptions to rules and exceptions to exceptions, each set up to provide for some case of suspected convenience.' Paul S Dunkin, who made this comment, records criticisms of ALA (1949) and appraisals of the LC *Rules for description* in his article 'Criticisms of current cataloging practice' *Library quarterly* 26 (4) October 1956 286-302. He points out the contrast in the two codes, 'twins by fiat of ALA', in that one (LC) looked ahead, and one (ALA) looked back. The LC *Rules* were based firmly on principles developed in a preceding study by Herman Henkle *Studies of descriptive cataloging: a report to the librarian of Congress* (1946), principles that called for a consideration of logical purpose linked with simplification and brevity (*eg* bibliographical elements in a book to follow a set order regardless of their appearance on the title page; author's name to appear only once in entry). LC *Rules for descriptive cataloguing: supplement 1949-51* (Washington, 1952), carried this trend further with such statements as that description should be limited to information readily available in the work being catalogued; that each new personal name entry would now be established in the form given in the work ... provided that it conforms to ALA entry rules and is not so similar to a previously established name as to give basis for suspicion that both names refer to the same person (the 'no conflict' policy); that the 1949 *Rules for description* should be applied only to reference works and scholarly and rare material, and that most other material should receive 'limited cataloguing' (*eg illus* to cover all kinds of illustrations).

Thus while the ALA *Rules* (1949) tended to reflect a traditionalist enumerative complexity, the LC *Rules* moved towards the increasing demands of cataloguers for more simplicity and brevity.

A D Osborn reviewed the ALA *Rules* (1949) very critically in 'ALA rules for author and title entries' *Library journal* 74 (13) July 1949 1012-1013, but found more to praise in the LC rules in 'Review of the LC 1949 code' *Library journal* 75 (9) 1950 763-64. J H Shera 'Review of the 1949 code' *Library quarterly* 20 (2) April 1950 147-50 noted, inter alia, the sheer growth in bulk of the rules. L Jolley 'Some recent developments in cataloguing in the USA' *Journal of documentation* 6 (2) June 1950 70-82, provided an authoritative assessment of the two codes, examining them carefully against the discussion and demands that produced them.

TOWARDS A NEW CODE

The 1949 edition of the ALA *Rules* did not produce an easy peace amongst cataloguers in the US or elsewhere. The American Library Association, in 1951, invited Lubetsky to prepare his critical study of cataloguing rules and in this same year the Library Association's Cataloguing Rules Subcommittee was re-convened for the first time since the second world war. H A Sharp 'Current research in cataloguing' in chapter two of *Cataloguing principles and practice: an inquiry* edited by M Piggott (London, LA 1954) pages 15-25, gives an account of the re-constitution of the Subcommittee and of the beginnings of a renewed collaboration of the two Associations with a view to producing a second Anglo-American joint code.

The British Subcommittee spent several not very fruitful years in consideration of the already obsolescent 1949 *Rules*. One development of note, however, was their decision, upon examination of those matters upon which the two Associations disagreed in 1908, to discard the British alternatives and to agree to follow the American rules as they appeared in the 1949 edition. Accounts of the LA Cataloguing Rules Subcommittee's work appear in *Library Association record* 57 (9) September 1955 352-353; 58 (7) July 1956 274; 60 (3) March 1958 89; 62 (8) August 1960 248-53.

As has been noted, Lubetzky's publication in 1953 of his *Cataloguing rules and principles* came out strongly against the codification of catalogue rules via the elaborate and complex enumeration of innumerable 'cases' and pointed a way towards the possible establishment of a less complex code based upon well-defined principles recognising more generalised 'conditions'. It was widely welcomed and Lubetzky was appointed editor of the new code. In 1957 his first drafts were received by the British Committee. Later drafts indicated that comments and suggestions made by the British Committee through correspondence had been taken into account.

In 1960 Lubetzky produced his *Code of cataloguing rules: author and title entry; an unfinished draft* (ALA 1960) which provided a radical new shape to the rules and in which the author wished to demonstrate a departure from 'formalism' to 'functionalism'. CCR was, like his previous work, generally welcomed by the progressives but there was evidence of worry on the part of those whom L Jolley has called the 'neo-conservatives', about such things as the probable costs of the extensive changes that would have to be effected in the catalogues if such rules were adopted.

One British librarian who has played a key role in rules revision is A H Chaplin of the British Museum, both by his participation in US cataloguing conferences (*eg* see his article 'A universal cataloguing code' *Library quarterly* 26 (4) October 1956 87-89) and in his function as organizing secretary of the International Conference on Cataloguing Principles held in Paris in 1961.

A draft statement of cataloguing principles based upon Lubetzky's *Code of cataloguing rules* was submitted to the conference for discussion along with working papers on the various problems of rules prepared by various delegates. A final version of the 'Statement of principles' was adopted and participants agreed to work in their various countries for revised rules which would be in agreement with the accepted principles.

Chaplin gives an interesting account of the events leading up to this conference, which resulted from a working group set up by IFLA in 1954 in ' International Conference on Cataloguing Principles 1: organization' *Journal of documentation* 19 (2) June 1963 41-45; while in the following article in the same issue L Jolley ' International Conference on Cataloguing Principles 2: thoughts after Paris', pages 47-62, provides a useful assessment of the conference with intelligent comment on the working papers. (He notes, wryly, that the statement of principles frequently manages to ignore the penetrating insights of some of these papers). Among points made by Jolley are that the statement of principles adopted is essentially the broad draft of an outline code; that it represents an international agreement so that future cataloguing developments must now take on an international context; that very broadly speaking it may be considered an endorsement of Lubetzky's work.

After this ICCP Conference, contact between British and American revision committees continued and increased. The Library Association has promoted two national conferences of cataloguers in London to discuss progress on the new code. A report of the first conference in July 1959 was published in the *Library Association record* 62 (8) August 1960 248-253. The second conference, held in May 1964, was reported by P A Hoare ' Cataloguing code revision: a participant's report' *Library Association record* 67 (1) January 1965 10-12. C Sumner Spalding, who succeeded Seymour Lubetzky as editor of the new code in 1962, was present and stated that there was a feeling in the US that Lubetzky's draft had insufficient detail to be suitable for research libraries and that he himself found it difficult to see things in the same way, and that it was decided to start again and re-draft, with emphasis on the Paris principles.

The US Code Revision Committee appears to have found itself in 1962 in the rather paradoxical position of having won international endorsement for the soundness and sanity of Lubetzky's *Code of cataloguing rules* and acceptance of his approaches as embodied in the Paris *Statement of principles,* while in the United States itself, the big libraries were viewing these two documents, in the light of possible cataloguing revision costs, with something less than enthusiasm. It would appear that at the Miami Conference of 1962, the Library of Congress and the Association of Research Libraries, having agreed on what they did *not* want the new code to do, were able to set limits to the extent to which the Code Revision Committee could apply the Paris principles, one result of which is found in the retention of the 'Institutions' entry, whereby many of these corporate bodies will continue (in the US version) to be entered under place. Lucile M Morsch 'An incubus and a hindrance' *LRTS* 11 (4) Fall 1967 409-414 reviews the relationships of the American Library Association with the Library of Congress over the years in the matter of rules revision, stating that certainly from 1949 onwards ' neither body was free to expand or modify any detail of its cataloguing rules without the specific approval of the other '. The *dominance* of the Library of Congress is evident in her statement that ' throughout the years of preparation there was a tacit understanding . . . that the new rules had to be satisfactory to the Library '. Miss Morsch sees this dominance as not only likely to continue, but to become even stronger in the future.

The British Cataloguing Rules Sub-Committees suffered from no such restrictions, except, perhaps, the obvious one that they were committed to working on what was to be a *joint* code and there is a limit (however imponderable) to the number of differences that can be accepted before two versions cease to be versions, and become separate codes. In the event, both texts (North American Text and British Text) of the new Anglo-American Cataloguing Rules were published in 1967, bringing to conclusion some sixteen years of work on the part of a large number of librarians in North America and Britain dedicated to the purpose of making library catalogues more effective and more efficient.

1967 AACR: *Anglo-American cataloging rules*: *North American text* (Chicago, American Library Association 1967).
*Anglo-American cataloguing rules*: *British text* (London, Library Association 1967).

While there is a strange echo of 1908 in that, once again, there *are* British and American differences, and while disparity might even seem to be confirmed by the fact that the two texts are physically very different in appearance, the British text printed on large paper having 216 rules occupying 327 pages, the North

American text in smaller format having 226 rules running to 400 pages, it would be a great mistake to read too much into the outer form.

The discrepancy in number of rules is accounted for by the fact that the British text omits two American rules (24, 99) in Part I (Entry and Heading) of the *Code*, and reorganises the enumeration of certain other rules in Part II (Description), *viz* seventeen British rules cover General Description of Monographs compared to twenty two American rules in the same section; Serials are covered by nine British rules compared to thirteen American, while there are six British rules for Incunabula compared to five American. But it must be said that, with certain exceptions, the differences between the two texts of the rules are most often a matter of rephrasing and reshaping statements rather than a matter of principles and practice. *Both* texts leave gaps in the numerical sequence of the rules achieving, in spite of the differences mentioned above, a high degree of parity in the numbering system.

AACR contains fifteen chapters arranged in three divisions. Part I 'Entry and heading' contains five chapters: entry; headings for persons; headings for corporate bodies; uniform titles; references. Part II covers 'Description' in four chapters: monographs; serials; incunabula; photolithographic and other reprints. Part III covers 'Entry and description of non-book materials': manuscripts; maps; motion pictures; music; phonorecords; pictures.

It is Part I, dealing with Choice and Form of heading in which the new Anglo-American rules present, most vividly, a new structured classificatory approach. Chapter 1 'Entry' substitutes categories or conditions of authorship in place of the preoccupation of earlier codes with the enumeration of types of works. Six general rules are established, then followed by more specific conditions, and this pattern of general rule preceding specific rule is successfully maintained throughout the code. Chapter 2 'Headings for persons' establishes the general rule that a person should be entered 'under the name by which he is commonly identified', and is followed by rules that apply themselves to classes of *names* rather than classes of *persons*. These rules, by and large, aim at establishing a 'user-oriented' heading, the heading that is most likely to be sought. Chapter 3 'Headings for corporate bodies' similarly aims at shaping the heading towards the catalogue-users' expectations, dropping previous distinctions between 'societies' and 'institutions', and directing that a corporate body be entered directly under its name, except when it is part of a higher body or an agency of government (although even in some of the latter categories, provision has been made for direct entry). Chapter 4 'Uniform titles' extends the practice (already widely accepted for such publications as music scores and sacred books) of collating works with variant titles under a uniform title.

Part II deals with Description, and while no really radical changes from the traditional elements and the order thereof is decreed, some modifications have been made, and it is in this section, particularly, that the greatest variation in phrasing and formulation of the rules between the British and North American texts obtains. The North American text concentrates on clarification and extension of the preceding LC *Rules for descriptive cataloguing*, while the British text, using the same base, has obviously attempted to depart from what has been called the 'US Governmentese' in which the prescriptions for producing printed card entries are laid down, making statements, less legalistic in style, which will cover descriptive cataloguing work in all kinds of catalogues.

In Part III, cataloguers have been provided with rules not only for maps and music, provision for which was previously made in LC *Rules for descriptive cataloguing* but also for the other major non-book materials. Part III deals with rules for both choice of heading *and* description for these materials, but the brief prefatory statement to this section in AACR states emphatically that the rules in Parts I and II apply to Part III 'to the extent that they are pertinent and unless specifically contravened or modified by the rules in the following chapters'.

Six appendices provide: a glossary of cataloguing terms; rules for capitalisation; abbreviations; numerals; punctuation and diacritics; and rules for entry and heading that differ in the two texts. The appendix in the British text contains the full text of the different American rules, unlike the American text, published earlier, which lists only the numbers of these rules. Neither text lists divergent rules in Description and Non-book materials.

The major point of difference occurs as a result of the inclusion in the American text of chapter 3 'Corporate bodies' of two rules for 'Exceptions for entry and place' whereby 'Local churches' and 'Certain other corporate bodies' (*viz* educational institutes, libraries, galleries, museums etc) will be entered under place, rather than directly under name. The American text, in a footnote, explains that these rules (which are essentially a continuance of the artificial 'Societies and institutes' practice of the preceding codes) 'are required primarily by the economic circumstances obtaining in many American research libraries. The cost of adapting very large existing catalogs to the provisions of the general rules for corporate bodies without such exceptions is considered to be insupportable.' In the British text the rule for 'Local churches' prescribes entry in accordance 'with general rules 60-64' and omits completely any rule for 'certain other corporate bodies' to be entered under place.

The above matter represents perhaps the only major conflict of principle between the two texts. Some lesser differences which may be noted occur with regard to: 'Designation of function' in heading (comp. ed. illus. etc) mandatory in the American text, optional in British text; rule 6, Serials, where rules in both texts specify successive entry in cases of changes of title, but a footnote indicates that Library of Congress will continue its practice of entry under latest title; rule 23, Court rules, with a somewhat more logical heading specified in the British text; rule 24, Annotated editions and commentaries, is omitted from the British text on the grounds that such editions are already covered by rule 11.

Among differences in descriptive rules may be noted: British rule 136 'statement of editor, compiler, translator etc' which provides for such statement to precede or follow the edition statement according to whether the editor etc is associated with the work or with the edition. (There is no 'editor statement' rule in the American text); variant specifications for insertion of reprint date (American rule 141, British rule 142); British provision for recording the number of plates (in as much as they represent leaves additional to the printed pages) immediately following the recording of the number of pages, in the statement of full pagination (Br rule 143 B); punctuation and diacritics (appendix V), wherein the American text simply lists the punctuation symbols and specifies the use of each throughout the body of the entry, while the British text more usefully enumerates the different parts of the entry and specifies at each point which punctuation symbols should be used.

F Bernice Field reviewed the new rules (American text) in 'The new catalog code: the general principles and the major changes' *Library resources and technical services* 10 (4) Fall 1966 421-436. The article summarises the main features of AACR and concludes that the rules 'will make catalogs easier to understand, to explain, and to use them at present. The cataloging process will be more reasonable because the rules are based on principles that are clearly explained instead of on precedents.' Michael Gorman 'A-A 1967: the new cataloguing rules' *Library Association record* 70 (2) February 1968 27-32 reviewed the British text at some length in the light of modern theory, finding some of the weak points as well as the strong points and deciding that the 'rules on *choice* of heading . . . are usually adequate and often very useful; the rules on *form* of heading or reference are rarely less than comprehensive and brilliant both in their wording and their results'.

A H Chaplin 'Cataloguing principles: five years after the Paris conference' UNESCO *Bulletin for libraries* 21 (3) May-June 1967 140-149 examines recent developments in cataloguing rules in many countries against the background of the Paris principles (a new version, '*Statement of principles. Annotated edition, with commentary and examples, by A H Chaplin assisted by Dorothy Anderson. Provisional ed* 1966' was issued by IFLA) and notes that, in the final result, correspondence between the AACR and the Principles is very close, although . . . 'both texts differ from the Principles (and from each other) in the criteria they apply for entering a serial publication under a corporate body'. He notes also that they introduce a new category of 'multi-author works' to be entered under editor, which category is not recognised by the Principles, which would require such works to be entered under titles.

As so often is the case in this era, the computer may have its say—even in the matter of rules revision. Phyllis A Richmond 'Commentary on three topics of current concern' *Library resources and technical services* 11 (4) Fall 1967 460-467 states: 'If computers live up to their promise . . . rules for entry, reclassification or subject heading changes could be done in one fell swoop (one swoop per change). These alterations would take extensive and expensive programming but the price would be small compared to the cost of changing manually. Lubetzky's logical rules may yet be adopted by courtesy of your friendly computer.'

READINGS

T E Allen and D A Dickman, editors *New rules for an old game* (London, Bingley 1968) contains *inter alia* papers by Lubetzky and F Bernice Field read at a two-day workshop on the AACR held by the University of British Columbia School of Librarianship in April 1967.

*Catalogue & index*: periodical of the Library Association Cataloguing and Indexing Group. Page 3 of issues 1-7, 1966-1967 records news from the LA Cataloguing rules Sub-committees.

P S Duncan ' Cataloguing and CCS: 1957-1966 ' *Library resources and technical services* 11 (3) Summer 1967 267-288. A useful overview of developments in both cataloguing and classification in the US. The section on ' Catalog code revision ', pages 276-279, should be noted.

C D Needham *Organizing knowledge in libraries* (London, Deutsch 1964). Chapter three, pages 30-39 ' Some existing English codes '.

C G Viswanathan *Cataloguing theory and practice* (London, Blunt third edition 1965). Chapter three ' Catalogue codes, origin, growth, development '.

37

# CHAPTER FOUR: COMPARISONS BETWEEN THE CODES

**C**OMPARISON of the rules in the various codes seems all too often to require unnecessary memorising of details that are, after all, readily available for consultation in the printed pages of these working tools of the cataloguer. But study of the comparative treatment of certain problems can lead not only to a better understanding of the problems themselves, but also to better evaluation and insight into the solutions proposed. Much work has already been done in this field (see the readings cited on page 48) and it is not necessary or desirable to survey all the rules in all the codes. The following is a brief tabulation of the main intent of the rulings of the five English language codes in respect of a representative number of problems.

JOINT OR CONTRIBUTORY AUTHORSHIP

BM 15: Enters both authors' names in heading in order of appearance on book. If more than two authors, under first named. Subsections provide for editor or title entry when more than two authors.

CUTTER 3-4: Enters only under first author named on title page. Reference from other(s).

AA 2: Enters two authors in the heading. If more than two, only first, followed by phrase '*and others*'.

ALA 3: Enters only under first author named on title page. Added entry for other(s).

AACR 3: Enters under the person or corporate body to whom *principal* responsibility attributed (by wording or typography). If no such principal author, enters under first named. Added entry for other(s) up to three authors. Over three authors, enters under editor or title.

UNCERTAIN OR UNKNOWN AUTHORSHIP

BM 18: Title to be basis of entry for anonymous works. Terms for heading to be selected from title in an order of priority *ie*

1 name of a person, 2 name of collective body or institution, 3 name of a place, 4 any other proper name, 5 first noun, 6 first word of title not article.

CUTTER 120: If author's name known, use it for main entry, otherwise under first word of title not article. Additional rules 121-132, for various cases of anonymity.

AA 112: Under name of author when known, otherwise under first word of title not article: AA 113-AA 118 cover change of title, initials, translators, etc. (Note US and British differ at 116 and 118.)

ALA 32: Enters under author when known, with added entry or reference under title. If author not known, enters under title, with added entry under phrase expressing authorship.

AACR 2: Enters under title, with added entry under an attributed author (if any). But, if reference sources indicate a probable author, enters under that person with added entry under title.

PERIODICALS

BM 17 C: Enters periodicals under form heading 'periodical publications' with the subheading being place of publication. Corporate publications under heading appropriate to society or institution.

CUTTER 133: Enters under first word of title not article. Two alternatives for change of title: 1 entry under successive titles with references, 2 under earliest with references.

AA 121: Enters under first word of title not article. In special cases, under society or body issuing it. Change of title produces different British and US rules: British under earliest title, US under latest title.

ALA 5 C: Enters under latest title. References or added entries for earlier titles. Periodical issued by corporate body ordinarily entered under title with added entry for body.

AACR 6: Enters under title. Exceptions allow for corporate entry and personal author entry under specified conditions. Successive entry recommended for change of title, or corporate names.

CHOICE AMONG DIFFERENT NAMES

BM 11: In case of authors who change their names, enters under original name as heading, affixing phrase 'afterwards' and subsequent name adopted.

CUTTER 40: Enters under 'best known form'.

AA 40: Alternative rules: British under original name following BM, US under latest form unless earlier decidedly better known.

ALA 45: Enters under adopted name unless original is decidedly better known.

AACR 40: Basic rule enunciates the principle of entry under the name by which most 'commonly identified'.

AACR 41: cites order of preference when doubt exists for personal name: (1) as generally identified in reference sources (2) most frequent form in works (3) latest form used.

AACR 62: cites a preference order for corporate names: (1) brief form (2) official form (3) predominant form (4) most recent form.

PSEUDONYMS

BM 20: Enters under pseudonym with affix *pseud* and real name added, if possible, in brackets.

CUTTER 7, 97: Enters under real name when known, *but* allows entry under pseudonym when 'writer habitually uses it or is generally known by it'.

AA 38: Enters under real name. If real name not known, under pseudonym with addition of *pseud* in heading.

ALA 30: Enters under real name when known. Exceptions allow for entry under pseudonym when real name unknown; when pseudonym has becomes fixed in literary history; when current popular authors better known by pseudonym.

AACR 42: Enters under pseudonym, if all works appear under it. If author uses several pseudonyms use name by which 'primarily identified'. In case of doubt, real name.

NOBLEMEN

BM 6: Enters under family name.

CUTTER 25: Enters under highest title, referring from family name, but, adds (rule 26), in the few cases in which family name or lower title is better known, enter under that.

AA 33: Differing British and US rulings: British under family name; US under title, unless decidedly better known by family name.

ALA 57: Enters under latest title, unless decidedly better known by earlier title or family name.

AACR 40: General rule of 'commonly identified' form would first be applied in choice between family name and title. Particu-

40

lar rule AACR 47 directs entry under title when author (1) uses title in works (2) is generally so listed in reference sources.

#### COMPOUND SURNAMES

BM 11: Enters under last part English (and Dutch) compound surnames. Other compound names adopted in entirety as headings.

CUTTER 28: Recommends last part for English surnames (when first has not been used alone by author); first part for foreign names.

AA 25: Enters under first part, unless author's own usage or custom of country makes exception advisable.

ALA 38: Enters under first part, with similar exception as in AA 25 above.

AACR 46 B: Cites order of preference for determination: (1) author's preferred form, or established form, if known (2) if hyphenated, under first part (3) normal usage in language of person involved.

#### SURNAMES WITH PREFIXES

BM 10: If English names, prefix treated as part of surname, and entry made under whole name. Specifies treatment for romance language names with, and without, the article.

CUTTER 29: If English, enters under prefix. French and Belgian under prefix when it is, or contains, article; under word following when prefix is preposition. In other languages, under part following prefix.

AA 26: If English, enters under prefix. Differential treatment for foreign names in general agreement with CUTTER 29 (Cutter drafted AA 26).

ALA 39: If English, enters under prefix. Gives clear rulings with good examples of cases in all other major languages.

AACR 46 E: Enters under element most commonly used in alphabetical listings in person's own language (shown, with examples, in the list of sixteen major language groups following). If, however, exceptional treatment is found in reference sources in the person's language, prefer such form.

#### CORPORATE BODIES: SOCIETIES

BM 5: Enters unofficial institutions, societies if they have national character under name of country, otherwise under name of town. *But,* international organisations, commercial firms, religious orders are entered directly under name.

CUTTER 61: Enters under their name as they read, referring from place of headquarters. Cutter's following rules—62-68, 71-74—deal with variations and exceptions.

AA 72: Enters under corporate name, with reference from place of headquarters. AA 73-81 deal with exceptions, variations etc.

ALA 91: Enters under latest corporate name, with reference from place of headquarters. Seven subsections to the rule deal with exceptions and variations.

AACR 60: Basic rule for all corporate bodies ('Societies *and* institutions') direct entry to be made directly under name, except when rules provide for entering it under name of corporate body of which it is a part, or under government of which it is an agency.

CORPORATE BODIES: INSTITUTIONS

BM 5: Enters institutions under name of state, province, town or other authority to which they belong. Museums, libraries, observatories etc, even if national in character, under name of place situated.

CUTTER 75-84: Enters institutions under place, allowing certain exceptions.

AA 82: Enters institutions under place located. AA 83-99 cover exceptions and special classes of institutions.

ALA 92: Enters under place located. Subsections and further rules 93-149 deal with exceptions, variations, further examples.

AACR 60: Basic rule as stated above applies to 'Institutions' also.

AACR 65 provides for addition of place-name to body if same name has been used by another body in a different location. American text (but not British) allows entry under place for local churches (American rule 98) and certain other corporate bodies (American rule 99).

CORPORATE BODIES: GOVERNMENT PUBLICATIONS

BM 5, 22, CUTTER 46-48, AA 58, ALA 72 all agree in their general rule that official publications should be entered under name of state, province, town or other authority to which they belong.

AACR 78: Provides for many corporate bodies (seven types being enumerated) created and controlled by government, to be entered directly under *their own names* in accordance with the general corporate body rules. The introductory note to the rule affirms the principle of entering only the basic legislative, judicial and executive agencies (parliament, ministries, departments etc) less directly *ie* as subheadings under the name of the government.

THE PROBLEM OF CORPORATE AUTHORSHIP

The above comparisons of the general corporate rules are arranged on the framework of the AA and ALA codes' oft-criticised distinction between societies and institutions, but, it should be noted, that BM and Cutter, while indicating that some corporate bodies should be entered under place, and others directly under name, do not attempt to categorise them so facilely with the two labels. Cutter, indeed, accused the BM of frequently avoiding the difficult issue of entry by its placing of so many corporate entries in ' a separate catalog' *ie* the form headings such as academies and congresses. Nevertheless, while his comments on corporate entry are basic reading, his rules do not really establish any clear-cut principles.

Lubetzky's chapter two, ' The corporate complex ' in his *Cataloguing rules and principles* (Washington, 1953) pages 16-35, reviews the numerous problems of corporate authorship, and on pages 48-55 he propounds such solutions as: 1 Enter under name of corporate body publications issued *in its name*; other publications under person or unit who prepared the work. 2 Bodies having a *generic* name common to many bodies of the same type should be entered under name of place, or under name of body with which it is affiliated. 3 Regard a change of name as the end of one body and beginning of another. 4 If a subdivision has a self-sufficient name of its own, it should be entered directly under its name. 5 In the case of an informal organisation, cataloguer takes the names of such corporate bodies as he finds them.

The International Conference on Cataloguing Principles was notably successful in gaining agreement on the principles of corporate authorship, especially since many countries (*eg* those oriented towards the *Prussian instructions* tradition) had for so long preferred to treat works by corporate authors as ' anonymous ' with main entry under title. The debate on corporate authorship (and the principles agreed) recorded in *International Conference on Cataloging Principles*: *report* edited by A H Chaplin and Dorothy Anderson (London Organizing Committee, c/o NCL 1963) pages 42-59, is worth reading on this point as are the two working papers on corporate authors by V A Vasilevskaya and Suzanne Honoré on pages 175-190. Vasilevskaya's paper includes a comparative survey of the treatment of corporate authors in many national codes.

R Taylor 'Corporate authorship and cultural evolution' *Library resources and technical services* 10 (4) Fall 1966 451-454 sees the emergence and acceptance of corporate authorship in the twentieth century codes, and at the Paris conference, as a gradual and progressive response of cataloguers from their original limited aim of bibliographical control in the library, through acceptance of the 'user-convenience' principle, thence towards international bibliographical standardisation. While the AACR 'potentially provides for the elimination of the archaic institution-society differentiation', Taylor believes that in retention of the certain exceptions (place-name for certain institutions') American cataloguers 'have failed (1) to recognise a higher cultural sanction than national self-interest (2) to accede to the user-convenience concept in practice . . . (3) to overcome . . . pecuniary interest and human laziness.'

ELEMENTS OF DESCRIPTION IN THE ENTRY

Many of the features of descriptive cataloguing have their origins in, and relate to, the practices established by the textual bibliographers. The objectives of the two disciplines are quite distinct, however, for while the textual bibliographer clinically analyses and carefully enumerates the components of the 'material object' he has examined for the purpose of giving a comprehensive anatomical description, the cataloguer is principally concerned with providing, within the array of entries in the catalogue, a statement sufficient in description to identify a copy of a book or document, to distinguish one edition of it from another, and to show its bibliographical relation to other books and documents.

Curiously, the commonplace terms, 'entry, main entry, added entry, heading' so frequently employed in the everyday work of cataloguers are not all that easy to use unambiguously in Anglo-American practice. Definitions of these terms might be compared in both texts of AACR where it will be found that *Entry*, in its primary usage, means the complete record of the bibliographical entity in the catalogue, but that it can also mean the heading under which the entry is made (American text) or, the aspect of cataloguing dealing with the choice of headings particularly for the main entry (British and American texts).

*Main entry* as 'the complete record of a bibliographical entity provided in a form by which the entry is to be uniformly identified and cited' is similarly defined in both texts, but the American practice of using the terms 'entry' and 'heading' somewhat interchangeably is reflected in a secondary meaning added to their definition.

In the present era, when unit entry is widely employed in catalogues *ie* when the same basic descriptive details are reproduced at various points in the catalogue under whatever headings the cataloguer selects, the utility of the concept of a 'main entry' has been questioned. More precisely, perhaps, it would be better to say the utility of the concept of 'main heading' has been questioned. In his paper on the *British national bibliography* at the Brasenose conference, A J Wells indicated that BNB intended to experiment with 'a form of entry that does not have a main entry heading.' He added, however, that since BNB is also used as a cataloguing guide, some way would have to be found of providing main entry heading information for those who consult the BNB for this purpose. A E Jeffreys 'Alternative headings' *Catalogue and index* (8) October 1967 4-5 also questions the validity of main entry in multi-access catalogues, suggesting that the unit card carrying full description, but without a built-in main heading, would permit more flexible arrangements of entries under any or all selected headings. He suggests that if a main heading is needed for any purpose that this could be done by adopting the convention of a tracing note which would list the main heading first on the list of tracings in every entry. C Sumner Spalding 'Main entry: principles and counter-principles' *Library resources and technical services* 11 (4) Fall 1967 389-396 in a searching analysis of what he terms the *four* principles (title, author, category, associated name) which may at one time or another be used in the selection of main heading in both AACR and the Paris principles (both of which are framed on the concept of main entry), notes 'The need for any entry to be chosen as a *main* entry depends on the fact that there are many situations in which that entry will be the *only* approach to the work . . . we are so used to multiple entry catalogs that we tend to forget the bibliographical situations in which there is only single access . . .

most union catalogues, many bibliographies, order lists, accession lists . . . in all bibliographical activities there is need for a standard mode of identifying works.' He further concludes that the dominance of the author principle in selection of main entry heading ' has not resulted so much from its intrinsic merit as a system . . . as from its great extrinsic merit of collation of works of each author as a by-product '. He sees its dominance thus being ' less a matter of its virtue as an abstract principle as it is a matter of pragmatic utility '.

The elements of an entry based upon AACR (British text) can be enumerated as *1 Heading 2 Description* which consists of (a) Title (including any sub-title or alternative title) (b) Author statement (c) Edition statement (d) Imprint; being the statement of place of publication, publisher, date (e) Collation; which cites the number of volumes (if more than one) or the number of pages and plates (if only one volume), followed by illustration details, followed by height of the work (f) Series statement. *3 Notes* of additional bibliographical information and/or specification of contents, if required.

The following features might be noted in the provisions made for description in Part 2 of AACR (British text):

AACR 133 B: *Long titles are abridged if this can be done without loss of essential information.* Carried over from the preceding RDC, this rule provides a welcome contrast to the venerable AA specification for ' title in full '.

AACR 113 E & F: Note the distinction between *alternative title* (always to be transcribed in full) and *subtitle* (being considered as part of the title may be abridged).

AACR 134: *Author statement.* F Bernice Field ' The new catalog code: General principles and the major changes ' *Library resources and technical services* 10 (4) Fall 1966 421-436 points out that restoration of the author statement in the body of the entry—the practice followed prior to 1949 was recommended by LC and accepted for two reasons: (1) the importance of having a record in the catalogue of the form of name appearing in the book (especially if it changes); (2) the author statement being the chief clue that identifies a new book with one already in the catalogue, in its absence, LC cataloguers were spending a great deal of time going back to the books. Author statement is provided for in AA 136 so that in theory (if rarely in practice) British libraries using AA should have included it. Both texts of AACR, however, allow for the omission in certain situations—the British text specifying the condition 'When an author's name is permanently associated with the catalogue entry whatever its function *ie* when there is a main author entry used in full as a unit entry'.

AACR 136: *Editor, compiler* etc. The statement of editor, compiler, translator etc to precede or follow the edition statement according to whether the editor etc is associated with the work or edition. A clear rule, not explicitly presented in the American text, although the practice is perhaps implied in the general principles of 'identification of edition' on page 191 of that text.

AACR 139: *Imprint*. The general rule includes provision for entering *without square brackets* any particulars, formally presented in the book, but not necessarily on the title page. This represents a distinct improvement over the venerable legalistic requirement whereby cataloguers had to insert the date in square brackets even if found on the reverse of the title page.

AACR 141: *Publisher*. Name to be given in the briefest form in which it can be understood and identified without ambiguity. Useful directions and examples follow this provision.

AACR 142: *Date*. Provision for insertion of a reprint date in parentheses after edition date, where the difference is important. All the major problems of entering dates are dealt with by direction and example.

AACR 143: *Collation*. Three elements are established to be clearly marked off with prescribed punctuation. (1) Statement of number of pages and number of plates (2) Statement of illustration with the permissive rule that 'illus.' may be used to cover all types of illustration. If the cataloguer considers particular types important they may be designated in *alphabetical* order from a given list of terms, although 'illus.' if included, will precede this designation. (3) Height in centimetres to nearest centimetre. The logic of supplying an accurate physical account of the book by stating the number of plates 'which do not form part of the sequence of pages' is indisputable. Whether the catalogue user will readily appreciate the nice distinction between what may appear to be a numbered statement of one type of illustration located along with the pages, while other types are arranged in alphabetical order in a separate sequence is perhaps debatable.

AACR 144: *Series statement.* In revising the rules, consideration was given to the possibility of placing this element, more logically, in the body of the entry, before the collation statement. This has not taken place, but some modest success might be claimed by the British Sub-Committee in as much as the American text also accepted the more logical designation 'Series statement' rather than 'Series note', and gave the rule separate status, in contrast to the earlier practice of simply including it in the section on notes.

AACR 145: *Notes.* The basic purpose of this section of the entry is to provide additional information *necessary* to the description, which cannot be provided in the body of the entry. AACR specifies clearly the 'purpose, forms, content and order' of such notes (the last section beginning with title notes and working logically through notes on various parts of the entry). Although some cataloguers have argued that bibliographies, if recorded at all, should be entered in the more formal part of the description, they are still to be listed under the contents note (145 c 9). It may be said, however, that this does give the opportunity to record, in pages, the *extent* of a valuable bibliography.

The tendency in descriptive cataloguing has been towards simplicity and brevity and away from rather pedantic pseudo-bibliographical style that 'full' cataloguing was often alleged to require. However, there is nothing new in this—Cutter's descriptive rules 223-297 recognised the requirements of 'short, medium and full' cataloguing and his frequent comments 'short will omit . . .' or 'I do not see why even full should use this . . .' are evidence of his thoughts in this direction, although these provisions for differential treatment were hardly conducive to the uniformity of practice nowadays sought. Mary Piggott 'Uniformity in descriptive cataloguing' *Libri* 13 (1) 1963 45-54 investigates the elements of description in different kinds of catalogues and national bibliographies, her article being written in the light of the agreements on choice and forms of heading at Paris in 1961.

READINGS

J C M Hanson *A comparative study of cataloguing rules, based on the Anglo-American code of 1908* (Chicago University Press 1939). Surveys, on the framework of AA *Code,* nineteen codes of rules including the BM rules (1927 edition), Cutter, and Vatican code (first edition 1931).

L Jolley *The principles of cataloguing* (London, Crosby Lockwood 1961). Chapter two, pages 12-55, 'The author catalogue', provides a penetrating commentary on ALA, AA and BM rulings for entry. Chapter three, pages 56-97, ' Corporate authorship ', gives a comprehensive exposition of this problem.

P R Lewis ' Points of departure: a first comparison of the 1908 and 1967 codes' *Catalogue & index* (9) Jan 1968 10-15.

C D Needham *Organizing knowledge in libraries* (London, Deutsch 1964). Chapters four and five, pages 40-63, ' The author approach ' and ' The title approach ', provide a survey of problems and code solutions analysed on the framework of Lubetzky's ' conditions '.

S R Ranganathan *Headings and canons: comparative study of five catalogue codes* (Madras, Vizwanathan; London, Blunt 1955). Compares Cutter, Prussian instructions, Vatican, ALA (1949) and Ranganathan's own Classified catalogue code.

H A Sharp *Cataloguing: a textbook for use in libraries* (London, Grafton fourth edition 1948). Chapters 23 and 24, pages 284-309, ' Comparative study of cataloguing codes '. Compares BM, Cutter and AA.

# CHAPTER FIVE: PROBLEMS OF SPECIAL MATERIALS

Libraries have for long included in their stock material other than printed books—manuscripts, maps and pictorial material being obvious examples. Newer forms of 'storable' records such as films and gramophone records, and variant forms of presentation of print such as microfilm, have emerged and proliferated in recent times, and many libraries have found it increasingly necessary to their purposes to widen their scope to include these and similar special materials. Consequently, cataloguing practice has been extended necessarily to include the listing and indexing of this special, or nonbook, material and to deal with the problems encountered.

Because these special materials are, in essence, similar to printed books in that they are records with intellectual content, there can be no fundamental difference in the application of general cataloguing principles to them. Differences centre more particularly on their variation in physical form, and some of the general problems emerging are:

1 Since a large proportion of the special materials do not have authors in the conventional sense, what element should be chosen for main entry heading? This 'author equivalent' is a most variable factor, ranging, for example, from the fairly obvious choice of composer in music scores, through title for films, to perhaps the cataloguer's own 'manufacture' as in the case of an untitled print or map.

2 Since their physical form or mode of presentation is frequently quite different from that of the book, which descriptive details are required in the body of the entry and how best can they be arranged and cited? The elements of the description, particularly the collation details, vary most widely in non-book materials and it is in this area, principally, that the cataloguer must develop special applications of general cataloguing practice.

3 Should the catalogue entries for these variant forms be included in the general book catalogue(s) of the library, or should

they be provided for in separate catalogues, indexes and lists? It is interesting to note that US practice has tended towards inclusion of special materials in the general catalogues, whilst European library practice has tended more towards the provision of the separate catalogues, lists or indexes.

This question of the desirability of separate catalogues and indexes is one of the recurring themes in an article by Jay E Daily ' The selection, processing, and storage of non-print materials: a critique of the Anglo-American cataloguing rules as they relate to the newer media' *Library trends* October 1967 283-289. The writer concedes that the rules in Part III of AACR which deal with non-book materials when ' viewed retrospectively as a summary . . . are superior ' but, in the course of the article, as he comments in turn on the rules for films, gramophone records, pictures, he criticises what might be described as the underlying philosophy of trying to tie the rules for such materials too tightly to the pattern established for books. He argues strongly for the treatment of ' each collection of non-book material as a separate and special entity, the use of which is inevitably governed by the nature of the material itself' and urges the use of book catalogues, edge-notched card systems or co-ordinate indexes using multiple entries as the occasion may demand.

FILMS

*Problems*: A basic problem exists in that reels and canisters of film cannot be scanned or handled in the same way as most other forms of record; consequently examination, even by the cataloguer for the purposes of cataloguing, must be kept to a minimum. This difficulty of physical accessibility to the record further imposes on the cataloguer the necessity of providing as far as possible all descriptive detail likely to be required by users, up to and including a summary or synopsis of content of the film record.

*Main entry heading*: Any film can be the result of the conjoint work of many diverse contributors, so films are most commonly identified by title, which is consequently the recognised element for the heading of the main entry. It should be noted, however, that a problem exists here in that titles can vary widely (or entirely differ) upon release of film in different countries (and so can the language in the sound track). AACR and UNESCO film catalogue rules prescribe entry under title of language version in hand, while the

ASLIB code (1963) recommends the establishment of heading under original title of release in country of origin.

*Description*: Following upon citation of title to which the designation (motion picture) or (film) is to be affixed, AACR specifies the following elements of description: production company and/or distributor; date; length *ie* running time (in minutes); sound or silent; b & w or colour; width (in millimetres); series statement; notes (*eg* change of title, versions etc); credits (producer, director, script writer, cast etc); summary (a descriptive factual synopsis of content, or in the case of fictional films, the plot).

*Subject cataloguing*: No essential divergence from conventional practice. The *British national film catalogue* (London, BNFC Ltd 1963- ) should be examined as an example of the classified form using UDC classification. The *Library of Congress catalog: motion pictures and filmstrips* (Washington, Library of Congress, 1953- ) has an alphabetical main entry section complemented by an alphabetical subject index based on LC subject headings. Both catalogues are bi-monthlies with cumulations. The indexing by producers, distributors, commentators, etc in BNFC should be noted. The headings in the LC catalogue are qualified by the descriptive phrases 'motion picture' or 'filmstrip' since they are based on printed card entries available for insertion in general catalogues. D Grenfell deals with the cataloguing of films in chapter twelve of J Burkett and T S Morgan *Special materials in the library* (London, LA (1963) pages 134-138, and the same writer's two articles 'Cataloguing of films' *Librarian* 47 (4) April-May 1958 62-64 and 'Standardization in film cataloguing' *Journal of documentation* 15 (2) June 1959 81-92 discuss the codification of film cataloguing practice, in which, it should be noted, there is no scarcity of codes, since Library of Congress rules (1958), UNESCO rules (1956), National Film Archive rules (1960) and ASLIB rules (1963) have all been formulated, with the above being joined by AACR (1967), Chapter 12, rules 220-229—replacing the Library of Congress rules.

MUSIC SCORES

*Problems*: Musical notation is a truly international medium, and works by the major composers have long been published in many countries by many publishers with title pages in many languages.

Many works have titles based upon their form, and popular titles as well (*eg* Beethoven's Sonata in C sharp minor, opus 27 number 2, is also popularly known as the ' Moonlight sonata '). Again, music publishers in every country have displayed a remarkable lack of uniformity in such matters as translation of the title or even the citation of the elements of it in any kind of standard order. Such matters have created for the music cataloguer a condition whereby the title page of the music score is not necessarily as sacrosanct as in other printed documents and, in fact, sometimes he may have to use it merely as a basis, deriving additional needed information from standard works of musicology.

AACR 233 recommends the establishment of uniform titles so that all variously titled editions and arrangements of a work may be collocated. The selection of the language for a uniform title can create a problem also, for whatever decision may be taken on the use of a particular language, there will be some works equally known and some perhaps better known by title in another language. AACR 234 recommends that ' the uniform title is established in the language of the original title, unless a translated title (in English or otherwise) is better known ' a rule that inevitably must put the burden of decision of ' better known ' form on the cataloguer.

*Description*: There is no essential disagreement among codes upon choice of composer as heading for main entry. It might be noted that AACR 19 B ' Librettos ' provides an interesting case study in the Anglo-American cataloguing rules. Rule AACR 19 for ' Other related works ' provides for entry of many related works (one and a half pages of examples) under their own author and title. AACR 19 B for ' Librettos ' is cited as an *optional* exception to this rule and permits entry under composer. A further subsection to AACR 19 B provides that if ' published as a literary work or without reference to a particular music setting, enter it under its author '. An example of open-ended provision, and also perhaps that the era of ' exceptions to exceptions ' is not yet ended.

TITLE: which may be the name of an opera or vocal work, or in the case of other musical works, may be composed of the following elements: form (*eg* sonata, trio, concerto, mass etc); form number (if any—sonata no 2, concerto no 8, etc); instrumentation or voices (' for violin, viola and 'cello ', ' for soprano and alto '); key (' in B flat '); opus number (this accepted musical convention for precise identification, though widely regarded as immutable, can be found to vary between one publisher's edition and another).

IMPRINT: The *publisher* is frequently important to the musician for identification of a particular edition wanted. The *date* is a relatively unimportant factor in scores and often enough is absent from the publication. AACR 245 D recommends, in the absence of a printed date, that a plate number or publisher's number should be added after the *supplied* imprint date.

COLLATION: *Number of pages, height* (in cms). AACR 246 B provides for the recording of parts, or score and parts in this section, noting that works issued in score only, should have the statement of the score included in the title transcript.

NOTES: Will be frequently used to elucidate the many features that can be present and may not be recorded in title *eg arrangements* ('orchestral work arranged for two pianos'; *language*(s) of works or libretto; *contents* of collections of pieces.

*Subject cataloguing*: Subject cataloguing of scores demonstrates the dominance of musical form, whereby entries are grouped under quartets, symphonies, concertos etc, frequently subdivided by instrumentation. The *Library of Congress catalog: music and phonorecords* (Washington, Library of Congress 1953- ) provides good examples of subject headings in its separate subject index, while the *British catalogue of music* (London, BNB 1957- ) bases its subject entries on a specially developed faceted classification scheme. A wide-ranging survey of the problems of music cataloguing can be found in International Association of Music Libraries *Code international de catalogage de la musique* (Frankfurt, London, Peters, two volumes 1957 and 1961) which has text in German, English and French. Volume one 'The author catalogue', surveys the comparative practice of a group of large libraries from many countries, and provides vivid illustrations of music cataloguing complexities in the form of twelve facsimile title pages, each exemplifying certain problems and accompanied by comparisons of the entries for these works in the various library catalogues. V Cunningham 'From Schmidt-Phiseldeck to Zanetti' *Notes* 23 (3) March 1967 449-452 reports on the work in volume three 'Code for full cataloguing' which contains rules for choice of heading, description, examples and an extensive glossary. An introduction discusses the principles upon which the rules are formed.

## GRAMOPHONE RECORDS

*Problems*: Obviously a repetition of those for music scores further complicated by the physical form of the sound record. The label and the sleeve provide the equivalents of the title page. (It should be noted that the sleeve often contains programme notes, lists of soloists, synopsis and much other needed information.)

*Description*: In addition to the details required for the citation of the music, elements of the gramophone record entry should include: imprint (name of *record company, manufacturer's catalogue number*); collation (*sides*—double or single, *size ie* diameter in inches, *speed ie* 33⅓ rpm 45 rpm etc, *kind of recording ie* microgroove, stereophonic); performance (orchestra, conductor, soloist, vocalist etc.); notes (contents of collections).

Chapter 14 of AACR 'Phonorecords', is not confined to rules for the gramophone record or disc but gives rules for description for the various physical forms of aural record (phonodisc, phonocylinder, phonotape, phonowire, phonofilm, phonoroll). The introductory note states that the term 'phonorecord' is used to fill the need for a single term to describe all types. Similarly, 'Phonodisc' has been selected as the most logical and convenient term to describe the record variously named phonograph record, gramophone record, disc etc.

Classification of the records is widely considered unnecessary in most collections, since users normally do not approach the shelves or containers for browsing as they can do with books. Accession number order, or even grouping by manufacturer's catalogue numbers can suffice on the shelves, and the catalogue must provide the mechanism for retrieval by 1 *composer* 2 *title* (note that a high proportion of records will have main entry under title since they can frequently focus on the nature of the music *eg* 'Folk music of Kashmir' or performer 'di Stefano sings Neapolitan songs') 3 *performer*. Added entries for soloists, conductors or orchestras should be made.

Since many records carry different works on each side, and can often contain many different items, analytical entries are frequently required. S A Somerville 'Cataloguing of gramophone records' *Librarian* 48 (5) July 1959 97-99 discusses record problems and gives examples of practice. The *Library of Congress catalog: music and phonorecords* (cited above) provides good examples of main entries and subject headings for gramophone records.

C Barnes ' Classification and cataloguing of spoken records in academic libraries' *College and research libraries* 28 (1) January 1967 49-52 describes some classification schemes for the material, and argues for the generous use of added entries in the catalogue. With regard to the question of entries being integrated in the general library catalogue or being filed in a separate catalogue, he states that the ideal solution is to do both.

MAPS

*Problems*: Maps have no title page in the conventional sense. AACR 212 B recomends that, while the title may be taken from any part of the face of the map, preference over a marginal title should be given to a title within the border of a map, or within a cartouche (the ornamental scroll with inscription often found on older maps).

AACR 210 and 212 in recommending main entry heading under person or corporate body responsible for the informational content (*eg* cartographer, publisher etc) seek a logical equivalent of book author in this way, but, except in the case of specialists seeking rare and antique maps, this is not a very common or probable approach by most map users. The British text of AACR provides a useful introductory note (not found in the American text) which bluntly states that most map libraries make main entry under the name of the area depicted, and that rules 210 and 211 determine the choice of entries which shall be compatible with author entries for books in an author and title catalogue. A footnote refers those seeking information on the use of area headings to the article by M E Fink (cited below).

*Description*: The details considered necessary for map entry will naturally vary with the nature of the library and/or the collection, but (following AACR 212) elements cited under heading may include: title; author statement; scale (expressed as a fraction *eg* 1 : 200,000); edition; imprint statement of place, publisher, date (note that there can be a difference between publication date and ' survey ' date, the latter, being important as indication of the state of the presented information, should be recorded in a note); collation statement—coloured (or otherwise); size (height by width in cms measured on outer edge of border); series statement. Notes may be used to indicate engravers, projection, survey dates, additional cartographic data.

*Arrangement of geographical headings*: Whether place names be used as main entry headings, or whether they be used for added entry headings for an alphabetical subject catalogue of maps, two different styles for these geographical or topographical map headings have emerged: specific geographical area versus a kind of alphabetico-classed geographical heading (*eg* continent-nation-state-locality). The latter scheme is considered effective for large collections, the Library of Congress Map Division being one example, and the kind of heading produced: Europe-Italy-Sicily-Palermo, produces a systematic arrangement within the entries. The specific entry principle (*eg* directly under Palermo) with connective references from some of the containing greater areas may be considered effective for the small collection, especially if the collection is mainly concerned with local maps and/or the entries are included in a general alphabetical subject catalogue. G R Crone comments on this point and indicates further subject subdivisions (geology, land use etc), as used in the catalogue of the Royal Geographical Society), in his chapter on maps in J Burkett and T S Morgan *Special materials in the library* (London, LA 1963) pages 92-94.

A concise summary of map treatment is also given in chapter one of Donald Mason *A primer of non-book materials in libraries* (London, AAL 1958).

Two useful articles are: B M Woods ' Map cataloguing: inventory and prospect' *Library resources and technical services* 3 (4) Fall 1959 257-73, which surveys the history and practice of map cataloguing during the present century, and M E Fink 'A comparison of map cataloguing systems' *Bulletin geog map division, Special Libraries Association* (50) December 1962 6-11, which compares features and practices of eleven map cataloguing schemes.

Automation of map collections and their cataloguing systems is indicated in such articles as C B Hagen 'An information retrieval system for maps' UNESCO *Bulletin* 20 (1) Jan-Feb 1966 30-35 where the classification elements and descriptive elements have been coded on 80-column cards, and W E Easton 'Automating the Illinois State University Map Library' *Bulletin geog map division* (67) 1967 3-9 where again using punched cards it is planned to produce a print-out book catalogue annually with monthly supplements.

MICROFORMS

*Problems*: The most fundamental problem is by no means confined to the cataloguing of the microform, but affects such aspects as storage, organisation and use. It is the variation in the *types* of microforms between transparent and opaque forms of different shapes and sizes. (*Microfilms,* in reels of different lengths with widths of 16mm, 35mm, 70mm; *microfiche,* transparent sheet film of various dimensions usually needing protective envelopes; *micro-opaque cards,* again of various dimensions, 5 × 3, 9 × 6 inches, which may carry images on one or on both sides.) The construction of an entry for a microform will naturally follow the cataloguing practice related to the original book or document of which it is a variant copy.

Description of the microform is entered *below the entry for the original*, which will have been entered according to the general rules.

*Description*: AACR 191 B cites the following elements; statement of type (microfilm, micro-opaque) followed by a statement of image, if negative, in parentheses; microform publisher, place and date; physical description, being number of pieces (cards, sheets, reels, containers) and size (width of reels in millimetres, height and width of cards and fiches in cms).

*Subject cataloguing*: There need be no essential difference in the subject cataloguing of microforms from those principles applied to books, and entries can be inserted in the general catalogue with the notes and details of the microform, drawing attention to their different physical form. But the question of how far analytical cataloguing should proceed in the case of microform publications containing voluminous works poses a fair problem. D T Richnell ' Microtexts: acquisition and organization ' chapter fourteen of J Burkett and T S Morgan *Special materials in the library* (London, LA 1963) pages 152-165, states this problem clearly, instancing a microprint publication containing more than 5,000 plays whereby, if each title were to be analytically catalogued, the library would have a major cataloguing problem on its hands. He concludes that libraries, in general, should avoid making the attempt to provide separate entries for items in *general* collections but rather should provide maximum publicity for the presence of such collections in the library. D Brockway 'A new look at the cataloguing of microfilm' *Library resources* 4 (4) Fall 1960 323-330, puts forward the view that too much descriptive detail concerning the original document tends to be inserted on the entry for the microfilm and such description should be limited.

OTHER MATERIAL

INCUNABULA (books printed before 1500) provide the cataloguer with the problem of producing entries based upon the practices of descriptive bibliography. Detailed analysis and recording of the features, physical and textual, of the particular copy is considered desirable for the purposes of possible comparison with other extant copies, and description should result in the careful transcription of the title page or colophon recording every detail exactly, down to the presence of printer's ornaments. The imprint will record *place of printing, printer's name* and *date of printing*. The collation should contain statements of *format; signatures; number of leaves* or *foliation; number of columns* per page; *number of lines* on page or column; *type area* in mms; *type style*. The presence of *capitals, catchwords, illustrations, printer's devices* must be indicated. The bibliographical note will cover description of the binding, peculiarities and imperfections of the copy catalogued, and references to the work in standard bibliographies of incunabula.

In view of the existence of such standard bibliographies, containing detailed descriptions of nearly all of the existing incunabula, AACR chapter 8 'Incunabula' formulates its rules on the basis that in a general catalogue only a short-title form of entry in conventional style will be required, the collation statement therein being followed by bibliographical reference (AACR 184), to a printed description in one or more of the published authoritative catalogues. The work by F R Goff *Incunabula in American libraries: a third census of fifteenth century books* (New York, Bibliographical Society of America, 1964) is particularly cited for this purpose. However AACR 185 (notes) does provide for such items as signatures and foliation to be specified, if they are not given in a cited source.

MANUSCRIPTS in a library may range from items such as literary mss, bound collections of an individual's letters, diaries etc having an author and a title page and to which 'conventional principles' can be applied, to miscellaneous documents and loose sheets such as wills, deeds, receipts etc, for which the cataloguer must supply a title and a summary of content sufficient for description. The 'book form' manuscripts can be dealt with generally in accordance with the rules for printed books so long as the entry clearly records in a note that the item catalogued is an original mss. The other forms of mss tend to force the catalogue to return to its historical origins and become more or less an inventory. A serial identity number may be supplied to each item and this may be used as the simplest basis of arrangement of the main entries, or, depending upon the nature of the collection, arrangement may be made under place or under date. In any case, special indexes covering names of persons, places, events will have to be provided to supplement the main entry sequence. The catalogue of such mss necessarily becomes a separate catalogue and is not usually compatible with the general library catalogue.

However, in chapter 10 'Manuscripts' of the AACR, emphasis is necessarily on compatibility with the general rules for printed materials (even if it may often result in the establishment of a heading by provision of what is merely an associated name). Rules 201 to 204 provide very well for the literary forms (medieval and modern); letters, speeches and lectures; legal papers; on the same principles of author and title entry developed in the general rules. (The principal examples for anonymous mss are to be found in the general rule 103, 'Works of unknown authorship without title'.) The form of the manuscript (holograph, ms, typescript etc) is to be shown in the first paragraphed note. Rules 205 to 207 provide for entry and description of collections of mss, establishing a preference order for main heading of (1) person or corporate body upon which collection is centred (2) collector's name (3) name of collection (if any) (4) title supplied by cataloguer. Michael Jasenas 'Cataloging small manuscript collections' *Library resources and technical services* 7 (3) summer 1963, 264-273 describes a scheme used at Cornell University whereby the cataloguing entry is focused upon the assembly of a 'cataloguable unit', consisting of gatherings of mutually related mss items.

ILLUSTRATIONS, PRINTS, SLIDES. Chapter 15 'Pictures, designs and other two-dimensional representations' of AACR provides, for pictorial materials, rules for 'standard catalogue entries which may be integrated ... in a general library catalogue'. The rules specify, predictably, entry under personal author (*eg* artist) or corporate body (*eg* printer, publisher, studio), and description entails such details as: title; author statement; place of publication; publisher; date (publication, execution etc); physical description—medium (an elaborate descriptive list of terms is supplied), colour, size (height by width in cms); notes.

But few illustration collections are limited merely to forms with such easily ascertainable details. More often, the picture collection will contain an extensive mixture of all kinds of pictorial material including photographs, illustrations clipped from periodicals, brochures (and even books), post-cards etc. In such collections, descriptive details in the entry as a means of approach to an illustration tend to be of limited value, and the main problem centres on the subject cataloguing method and subject arrangement of the material. In fairness to AACR, it must be said that the introductory notes to the chapter recognise this fact—'most pictorial works in libraries may be economically and efficiently serviced by arrangement in files by subject or other category ... in accordance with the needs, size, and specialisation of a particular library, some of the descriptive details may be either simplified or elaborated and the number of added entries increased or decreased'. C H Gibbs-Smith 'Visual materials' chapter eleven, pages 117-126, of Burkett and Morgan's *Special materials in the library* describes the system used in the Hulton Library based on four subject groups (portraits, topographical, historical, modern) and questions the need for 'card indexes', on the presumption that the scheme should be self-indexing. D Mason's 'Illustrations' chapter two of his *Primer of non-book materials* (cited below) mentions a comparable broad scheme used in the New York Public Library (views, personalities, general) but also instances collections classified by DC with subject indexes.

D Rogers 'Works of art' *Catalogue and index* (5) Jan 1967 4-6, and, (6) April 1967 10-11 deals in depth with the requirements of cataloguing original works of art, finding it necessary to specify more descriptive elements than are provided for in AACR.

A useful article on the rather difficult problem of cataloguing SLIDES is Peter Havard-Williams and Stella A Watson 'The slide collection at Liverpool School of Architecture' *Journal of documentation* 16 (1) March 1960 11-14, which describes how, with the slides arranged in accession order, cataloguing rules were formulated with the necessary emphasis on the subject catalogue and subject headings. A scheme of descriptive details used is given, but it is stated that, in practice, it was found that elaborate descriptions were unnecessary. B W Kuvshinoff 'A graphic graphics card catalog and computer index' *American documentation* 18 (1) Jan 1967 3-9 describes a card catalogue for slides and photos in which the cards carry miniature reproductions of the pictorial material, visible data entered by typewriter, and coded data keypunched. The cards can thus be manually searched, and employed for various other manual applications, while a computer can be used to prepare indexes from the punched data.

READINGS

J Burkett and T S Morgan eds *Special materials in the library* (London, LA 1963). A collection of fourteen lectures by specialists on the treatment of special materials which clearly indicate the diversity of their approaches to the various problems, including cataloguing.

Thelma Eaton *Cataloguing and classification: an introductory manual* (Illinois, Illini Union Bookstore, third edition 1963). Chapter seven, pages 138-155, 'The organisation of special materials', considers the problems from heading through to collation, illustrated with several facsimile entries of LC cards based on the various LC rules for special materials.

E Hensel ' Treatment of nonbook materials ' *Library trends* 2 (2) October 1953 187-197.

Donald Mason *A primer of non-book materials in libraries* (London, AAL 1958). Sections in each chapter deal with the cataloguing, or arrangement and indexing, of the principal special materials.

D M Norris *A primer of cataloguing* (London, AAL 1952) chapter ten, pages 142-172 ' Cataloguing of special collections '.

Brian Redfern *Organizing music in libraries* (London, Bingley 1966). Chapters four and five are devoted to cataloguing of music, and chapter six to gramophone records.

# CHAPTER SIX
# INNER FORMS OF CATALOGUES

A catalogue is, by definition, a list of books in a library or collection, the entries in the list being arranged in some systematic order. This order, or mode of arrangement, determines the 'inner form' of the catalogue.

The *author catalogue* is a catalogue with, in the main, authors' names in the headings, arranged alphabetically. The entries will, however, usually include those for editors, translators etc and, for certain works (*eg* serials, anonymous works) title entries. Added entries for significant titles are usually included in this sequence so that, most usually, the form of catalogue should be designated as an *author/title catalogue*. Identification of a book or document by means of named author is such an obvious and traditional approach by users of libraries, that there is little dispute about the primacy and importance accorded to the author catalogue as a form, and it still remains the chief object of attention in the catalogue codes. While some libraries manage to get along without a subject catalogue (or with only a very imperfect version of one), none can properly afford to dispense with the author or author/title approach.

The description *subject catalogue* may be given to any catalogue in which the headings on the entries designate the subject matter of the work and the entries are arranged systematically for subject identification and retrieval. If the headings are words, terms or phrases and are arranged alphabetically, the catalogue is an *alphabetical subject catalogue*. If such subject headings are selected to indicate as precisely as possible the 'specific subject' of the book or document and are linked with connective references between related subjects, the catalogue may be described as an *alphabetico-specific* or *alphabetico-direct catalogue*. If the headings are classification symbols arranged in accordance with the sequence of the classification scheme (preferably complemented with an alphabetical index of subjects), the catalogue is then a *classified subject catalogue*.

A subject catalogue which has been claimed to represent a compromise between the alphabetico-direct and the classified forms is the *alphabetico-classed,* in which the entry word of the heading consists of selected broad class terms or generic subjects. The subject specification is cited in the accompanying sub-heading. Arrangement throughout is alphabetical. The alphabetico-classed catalogue cannot be accepted as a viable form for contemporary use, having more or less vanished in the nineteenth century. The BM *Subject index* has been frequently cited as an example by some writers, but L Jolley *Principles of cataloguing* pages 109-110 shows that no such pattern was in the mind of the original compiler, G K Fortescue. (R Bancroft ' The British Museum subject index ' *Indexer* 3 (1) Spring 1962 4-9 attempts to explain BM practice, stating that the arrangement is alphabetical by subjects, *some* of which are subdivided.) No perceptible principles can be detected in the mixture of broad and specific headings chosen in any volume and, in accordance with a policy of ' decentralization of certain headings ', headings have tended to vary in each five-yearly issue.

A variant form of catalogue, whose use has been more or less confined to Britain, is the *name catalogue.* The headings on the entries are those of proper names of persons and places and include both works ' by ' and works ' about ', the entries being arranged in one alphabetical sequence. Some versions are restricted to personal names only. It amounts to an author/title catalogue with that part of an alphabetical subject catalogue relating to proper names added, thus providing partial subject coverage. The value of varying versions of this form of catalogue, which has sometimes been used in conjunction with a classified subject file (in lieu of an alphabetical subject index), has not been satisfactorily proved.

The provision of the author/title catalogue form in conjunction with two of the subject catalogue forms (alphabetico-direct in the one case and classified in the other) produces the two ' classical ' inner forms of full library catalogue. These are:

1 The *dictionary catalogue,* which inter-files its author/title headings, specific verbal subject headings and connective references in one alphabetical sequence;

2 The *classified catalogue,* in which the principal component is the classified file of subject entries, complemented by alphabeti-

cally-arranged indexes of subjects, authors, titles. These indexes may be arranged in a single, or in separate, alphabetical sequence and the author/title index may be a full author/title catalogue or may be more restricted in bibliographical detail than the full entry in the classified file.

Of the two forms, the classified catalogue has the longer history, probably deriving from the original 'inventory' function of the catalogue whereby, as the books in the old libraries were grouped in broad categories of knowledge and press-marked, the inventory of the book store consequently followed some systematic order of knowledge, however crude. The pattern of systematic arrangement of entries in accordance with a classified order of knowledge became and remains a strong tradition in the libraries (and subject bibliographies) of Europe and Britain to the present day, and although the early shelf-lists would have lacked the complex notation, added entries, and indexes, of the present-day catalogues, they provided the basis for such later developments.

The dictionary catalogue came on the scene much later, and emerged in the United States towards the end of the nineteenth century. Alphabetical subject indexes of a sort had been produced in Europe, but the headings were usually limited to words selected from the book title (catchwords, or keywords) and the codified practice of establishing a specific subject heading in words not necessarily derived from the title-page, had to wait for Cutter's *Code* of 1876. After Cutter, the dictionary catalogue became the almost universally accepted form of catalogue in the American scene and, indeed, was introduced widely elsewhere. The classified catalogue was ousted almost entirely in the United States, but the new method was not so completely accepted in Europe where both forms co-exist today.

The existence of these two forms of subject catalogue has provided a continuing debate among librarians on the relative merits and shortcomings of each form. It is perhaps a tribute to the qualities of *both* forms (if not merely to the conservatism of cataloguers) that, with so much analysis and appraisal being directed at the comparison over such a long period, and with so many librarians with strongly-held convictions participating in the debate, that the situation has remained so little changed throughout the years.

The sections on the dictionary catalogue and the classified

catalogue in chapter twenty five of H A Sharp *Cataloguing* (London, Grafton, fourth edition 1948) give an historical account of catalogues representative of each form, while John Metcalfe in *Subject classifying and indexing of libraries and literature* (Sydney, Angus and Robertson, 1959) pages 38-43 gives a somewhat opinionated explanation of the history of the divergence in subject catalogue form throughout the library world. J McRee Elrod ' The classed catalog in the fifties' *Library resources* 5 (2) Spring 1961, 141-156 reviews attitudes to the classified form on a continental basis, indicating its supremacy in Europe and stating that there are indications in the USA of a willingness to study this form.

THE CLASSIFIED CATALOGUE AND SUBJECT INDEXING

The use of the notation of the classification scheme in the headings to arrange the subject entries produces a systematic array and logical collocation of subjects derived from the schedules of the chosen scheme. Approach to the subject file can be made directly if the notation for the required subject is known by the user, but most usually, the approach must be made via an alphabetical subject index which should translate the terms of the subject sought into a class number.

Melvil Dewey's 'Relative index', by introducing the practice of qualifying any index term sought by such terms as were indicative of any phase or aspect of it in the classification schedules, laid the foundations of modern subject indexing. He realised that the classification schedules often must separate, quite logically, related topics under different generic classes, and that it should be the function of an index to collect such distributed relatives under the sought term. Ranganathan developed this practice further with his ' chain procedure', which systematises the method of preparing subject index entries for the classified catalogue by analysing each component part of the chosen class mark into a series of terms describing the specific subject, and the successive containing classes from which it descends in the classification hierarchy. Each term in the ' chain ' thus obtained, successively produces an index entry, qualified if necessary by one or more of the containing terms to indicate the context.

Ranganathan had first mooted this method as early as 1938 in his *Theory of library catalogue* (subsequently developing it in later editions of his *Classified catalogue code*) but it was not until the publication of B I Palmer and A J Wells *The fundamentals of library classification* (London, Allen and Unwin, 1951) and more particularly, with the introduction of chain indexing into the *British national bibliography* in 1950—that the method became widely known and accepted in Britain. There is no doubt of the profound effect it has had since upon the theory and practice of the classified catalogue in Britain and, to some extent, abroad. The success with which BNB, over sixteen years, has applied this subject indexing method and other devices such as 'feature headings' to a huge national bibliography arranged in the form of a classified catalogue, has produced fresh appraisals of the effectiveness of this form of subject catalogue and caused even its most severe critics to look at it again. A basic account of chain indexing is J Mills 'Chain indexing and the classified catalogue' *Library Association record* (57) 4 April 1955 141-8, while E J Coates *Subject catalogues: headings and structure* (London, LA, 1960) gives an account of chain indexing in BNB in the chapter on 'Chain procedure applied to the decimal classification' pages 119-131.

THE FEATURES OF THE CLASSIFED CATALOGUE

1 Arrangement of subjects in the classified file is logical and systematic. Co-ordinate and subordinate relationships of subjects are displayed within the framework of the classification schedule providing for a systematic survey of related subject areas.

2 Subject index complements the classified file by collecting under the sought term all aspects of the subject including those which have been logically separated in the classification scheme. Such an index can aid in the formulation and clarification of the subject search.

3 The notation used to arrange the subject file provides a language independent of natural language, free from many of its difficulties, and more accessible to users on a multilingual basis.

4 Subject index provides for flexibility of additions, corrections, and revisions of subject terms with minimum of effort and no dislocation of subject file. Synonymous terms may be directly indexed to class number and referencing is minimal.

*Criticisms* that can be made include:

1 Classified file of subject entries reflects any illogicalities

present in the classification scheme. Again, with the advance of knowledge, parts of the schedules may go out of date, necessitating revision of the relevant part of the subject catalogue.

2 The notation in the headings of the classified file is not as readily acceptable and comprehensible to the average user as verbal subject headings.

3 Approach to the required subject entries must, in most cases, be an indirect two-step process, because of the need to use the alphabetical index.

4 User does not always require the complete classified sequence of associated subjects, but, quite often, simply wants material on a specific subject quickly.

A comprehensive tabulation and comparison of the pros and cons of the classified catalogue and the dictionary catalogue is provided by J H Shera and Margaret E Egan *The classified catalog* (Chicago, ALA, 1956) pages 14-21. C D Needham *Organizing knowledge in libraries* gives a brief assessment of the classified catalogue on pages 128-129 and the alphabetico-direct and dictionary form on pages 140-146.

THE DICTIONARY CATALOGUE AND SUBJECT HEADINGS

The alphabetico-specific subject catalogue, which is a basic component of the dictionary catalogue, aims at establishing a verbal subject heading which will be exactly descriptive of the content of the document identified. Cutter's basic rule 161 ' enter a work under its subject heading, not under the heading of a class which includes that subject ' states in these simple terms the basis of dictionary catalogue practice. If natural language permitted the establishment of headings for all possible subjects in uncomplicated and unambiguous terms, or brief phrases, without possibility of conflict between cataloguer and catalogue user, the task would be a simple one.

However, Cutter saw many of the problems that immediately arise, *eg* complex topics stated in lengthy phrases that have yet no brief ' established ' name; compound or overlapping subjects; synonyms; conflict between topic and locality; and he gave the best directions he could conceive towards their solution, such as advocating direct entry (without inversion of terms) under the most commonly accepted name for a subject. He also laid down the basis of the ' syndetic ' structure of the catalogue, by directing that references should be made downwards from generic or containing classes and collaterally from co-ordinate subjects, and by this method the subject catalogue claims to connect interrelated subjects logically, and facilitate a subject search independently of any classification. US dictionary catalogue practice is still largely based on his precepts, and the Library of Congress *Subject headings list* and Sears' *List of subject headings* (which derives from it), as working tools for subject heading practice, reflect Cutter's rules. Sears' list is intended for small and medium size libraries and, on this ground, omits many specific headings which the LC list requires, but *both* lists of headings and recommended references reflect many of the inconsistencies that have grown up through the years as a result of difficulties which Cutter was unable to resolve.

D J Haykin *Subject headings: a practical guide* (Washington, Library of Congress, 1957) attempts to state the principles upon which the LC list operates but E J Coates *Subject catalogues* page 66 remarks 'Little or no attempt has been made to keep theory abreast of the developing practice, with the result that the present day LC *Subject headings* appears to embody a large number of purely arbitrary decisions . . . which do not form anything approaching an overall pattern of practice'. Confirmation of this particular criticism can be found from a somewhat unexpected source, a writer who has continually expounded on the virtues of verbal subject headings. J Metcalfe *Alphabetical subject indication of information* (New Brunswick, Rutgers University Press 1965) states (p 18) that Cutter's rules for the dictionary catalogue is the only generally known or recognised code but there has been no edition or revision since 1904 and they do 'not meet the need of sixty years later . . . for good and ill they are no longer strictly followed. The basis of present practice of alphabetico-specific entry is mainly a vague understanding of its basic concept'. A comparison of the two lists of subject headings was reported by Sydney L Jackson 'Sears and LC *subject headings*: a sample comparison' *Library journal* 86 (4) February 1961 755-756, 775 in which it was concluded that the more specific subject headings omitted by Sears would not prove to be disruptive if used in the catalogues of smaller libraries. M F Tauber 'Subject headings and codes' *Library resources* 3 (2) Spring 1959 97-102 suggested the need for a national subject headings code to supplement Cutter's rules and indicated that a study of basic principles was a necessary preliminary.

The latest edition of *Subject headings used in the dictionary catalogs of the Library of Congress* (seventh edition 1966) has been most efficiently produced by the combination of computer processing, automatic photocomposition and offset process, and as a result of the automated printing techniques developed, it is promised that subsequent new editions will be more up-to-date and more quickly produced than ever before. But there are some indications that the *nature* of the product should be looked into more closely and perhaps subjected to similar systematic analysis. S L Jackson 'Long files under LC subject headings, and the LC classification' *Library resources and technical services* 11 (2) Spring 1967 243-245 cites some LC subject headings which are not subdivided (selected from LC Catalog: Books Subjects. 1950-1959) and states that, under such headings, many library catalogues will have long files (upwards of 200 entries) in a single author-alphabet, discouraging to the searcher. He suggests that this condition obtains 'partly because the Library of Congress classification frequently affords more specific subject approaches to the material than its subject headings are capable of'. He indicates the need for such headings to be refined by LC, or for the particular libraries to subdivide such accumulations on the basis of the LC class numbers on the entries filed under these headings. The writer concludes 'Two things are reasonably clear: subject files exceeding two hundred entries in a single author-alphabet are dubious assets, and the prospective automating of cataloguing from LC copy will not of itself solve the problem'.

J Kaiser in his *Systematic indexing* (London, Pitman, 1911) has been recognised as having made a significant contribution to the theory of subject headings, even though his approach was from the viewpoint of information indexing rather than book and document cataloguing. He proposed a procedure for breaking down subjects into two elements, 'concretes' and 'processes'; systematically trying to formulate headings as 'things', 'places', etc (the concretes) qualified by 'actions', 'activities' (the processes) expressed, or implicit in the concept. J Metcalfe *Subject classifying and indexing of libraries and literature (op cit)* pages 297-300 devotes an appendix to a description of Kaiser's work and theories. A paper by Kaiser on his systematic indexing given at a 1926 ASLIB conference is reprinted in R K Olding *Readings in library cataloguing* (see page 20).

E J Coates in his work on *Subject catalogues* already cited, not only analyses the approach of Cutter, Kaiser and others to the problem of verbal headings (chapters 4 and 5, pages 31-49) but also develops his own theory for the formulation of headings for compound subjects on a 'significance order' of thing-material-action. He examines the relationship between the elements in some twenty compound subject 'conditions' and, on the basis of his theory, gives a table of relationships, establishing a logical order of the components for the composition of the subject heading. Coates' work is important, not only as a penetrating analysis of the structure of the alphabetical subject catalogue and the problems of subject specification, but also because, as editor of *British technology index* (1962-) he has been able to translate his theories into practice in the headings created therein. The indexing method used in *British technology index*, as well as other various indexing methods and their associated problems, are discussed by Coates in 'Scientific and technical indexing' *Indexer* 5 (1) Spring 1966 27-34.

### THE FEATURES OF THE DICTIONARY CATALOGUE

1 A single sequence of author/title/subject headings in alphabetical order is easily comprehensible to the user since it reflects the pattern established by dictionaries, encyclopedias, etc.

2 The single sequence permits ease of consultation, while the specific heading facilitates quick reference. The 'syndetic' chain of subject references gives 'lead-through' from generic to specific subjects and from collateral subjects.

3 The subject headings are independent of any classification scheme used, and thus there is freedom to establish headings which will collect related material which has been separated in various classes in the classification schedules.

4 Subject headings can be shaped to match the user's terminology.

*Criticisms* that can be made include:

1 Verbal subject headings also separate related classes and subjects and 'scatter' them through the array of catalogue entries on the basis of their accidental occurrence in the alphabet.

2 The network of references and cross-references can be often bewildering to the user.

3 Dependence upon a list of 'established' subject headings leads to difficulties with semantic change and obsolescence of terms.

4 The allegedly simple alphabetical sequence of author-title and subject headings can become extremely complex as the catalogue grows and can lead to difficulties in both filing and retrieval.

This latter difficulty has resulted in certain US academic and other large libraries 'dividing' their catalogues into separate author/title and alphabetical subject sequences on the grounds of relieving congestion, lessening complex filing problems, increasing ease of consultation, producing a better physical lay-out for the catalogue. This step, however, is a fairly fundamental reversal of the principle of the classic form of the dictionary catalogue and does not seem to meet with universal approval. The chapter on 'The divided catalogue' pages 92-101 in M F Tauber *Cataloguing and classification* (volume one, part one of *State of the library art*—New Brunswick, Rutgers University Press, 1960) gives a concise summation of the US position on this matter. The chapters in the same work on 'The dictionary catalog' pages 65-77 and 'The classified catalog' pages 78-91 provide a useful summary of opinion on these forms derived from the literature up to the late nineteen fifties, while part 2 of the volume (Carlyle J Frarey *Subject headings*) is devoted to a wide-ranging review of developments in this area.

Perhaps the most curious feature of the US subject cataloguing scene is the bland (almost complacent) acceptance of the fact that the verbal subject headings presented in LC and Sears lists, from thence being employed in the dictionary catalogues of countless libraries, rest upon no body of logical and consistently-applied principles. This situation is well-described in the section on 'Subject headings' of the article by P S Duncan 'Cataloguing and CCS: 1957-1966' (already cited above, *see* page 37) and a few random quotations from this summary of nine years developments may illustrate the point. 'Both lists (LC and Sears) still suffer from our preoccupation with the " convenience of the public " inherited from Cutter . . . Haykin's work was only an attempt to arrange inherited practice into a logical system . . . specificity is a magic word which we all accept but seldom really define . . . John Metcalfe's *Alphabetical subject indication of information (1965)* is incoherent but stimulating . . . as the ten years ended Richard Angell was appointed Chief of the newly created Technical Processes Research Office in LC. Perhaps LC will do some re-thinking of subject heading theory.'

The fact that LC presently bids fair to become the automated bibliographic centre of the world, places such uncertainty about its subject cataloguing theory and practice, and about its intentions in this area, in rather odd perspective.

READINGS

The works by E J Coates *Subject catalogues: headings and structure* and J H Shera and M E Egan *The classified catalog* already cited in the body of the chapter provide basic reading. J Metcalfe *Subject classifying and indexing of libraries and literature* (Sydney, Angus and Robertson 1959) chapter 8 ' The classified catalogue ' and chapters 11 and 12 ' The dictionary catalogue ' are useful, although the whole work is somewhat marred by the author's commitment to the alphabetical subject catalogue being carried as far as abuse of Ranganathan, BNB, and other theories or practices which conflict with his own views. The same author's *Alphabetical subject indication of information* (New Brunswick, Rutgers University Press 1965) contains much useful information on subject heading theory although it somewhat belies its series title ' Rutgers series on systems for the intellectual organization of information ' in not being a very well organised document.

*Other readings*
L Jolley *The principles of cataloguing* (London, Crosby Lockwood 1961) chapter 4 ' The subject catalogue '.
Margaret Mann *Introduction to cataloguing and classification of books* (Chicago, ALA second edition 1943). Chapters 9 and 10 deal with dictionary catalogue, subject headings, and Sears and LC lists.

# CHAPTER SEVEN

# PHYSICAL FORMS OF CATALOGUES

THE manner in which the library catalogue can be made available for use by the reader has produced a number of 'physical forms' of presentation.

THE PRINTED BOOK CATALOGUE
In this the entries are printed as text in a conventional book-form catalogue available in multiple copies.

*Features*: It is the easiest form of catalogue to use, and the most acceptable and comprehensible to the greatest number of people. It can be guided with great clarity by manipulation of typography and layout. A printed page of entries can be scanned with greater speed and less error than any other arrangement, and its 'portability' and multiplicity of copies offer great advantages.

*Problems*: It is highly expensive when produced by conventional printing methods and, in a growing collection, is out of date immediately. It offers no possibility of insertion or interpolation of entries for new material, which can be indicated only by way of supplements, and this then produces the problem of 'several places to look'. The problem of 'withdrawals' can only be met by producing new editions at regular intervals.

The printed book catalogue as a viable form appeared to die the death in the early years of this century when, in libraries large and small, it was replaced by the new more flexible card catalogue. Yet, technological advance appears to be turning the wheel full circle. Newer methods of printing allied with photography and offset lithography have shown that the entries on cards or slips in the catalogues of large research libraries or collections (with little or no withdrawal problems) can be efficiently transformed into book-form catalogues, as has been done on a fairly extensive scale by the G K Hall Company for the catalogues of many specialised libraries and collections and, on an even larger scale, by Mansell for the catalogues of the British

Museum and the *National union catalog: pre-1956 imprints*. The availability of such catalogues in book form has added a new dimension to the bibliographical apparatus of libraries acquiring copies. It also led to many large libraries considering the possibility of reducing the bulk of their card catalogues at a certain date to book form, and perhaps supplementing this with entries in a card catalogue. Again, the computerised cataloguing system, with its ability to store entries, to interpolate new entries, erase withdrawals and produce printed-out up-dated versions of the catalogue in book form at suitable intervals, has led to a revival of the oldest form of catalogue by means of the newest method of preparing catalogues. J H Shera ' The book catalog and the scholar: a re-examination of an old partnership' *Library resources* 6 (3) Summer 1962 210-216 states that the card catalogue ' has reached the point of dimishing returns ' and discusses the possible return of the book catalogue produced by non-conventional printing methods. In the same periodical and issue, pages 217-222, M R McDonald ' Book catalogs and card catalogs ' echoes this theme—' the card catalogue is doomed to destroy itself '—offering the solution of the book catalogue supplemented by card catalogues.

F A Sharr ' Book-type catalogues for developing countries ' UNESCO *Bulletin* 20 (1) Jan-Feb 1966 24-26 and ' The production of a new book-type catalogue in Australia ' *Library resources and technical services* 10 (2) Spring 1966 13-14 has described how the book form catalogue for the Western Australia State Libraries, is produced without using particularly expensive equipment, by means of short entries typed on Kalamazoo Copystrip and reproduced from litho plates. Typical of the veritable spate of articles on the computerised book catalogue is perhaps C W Robinson ' The book catalog: diving in ' *Wilson library bulletin* 40 (3) November 1965 262-268 and P Kieffer ' The Baltimore County Public Library book catalog' *Library resources and technical services* 10 (2) Spring 1966 133-141, both of which deal with the production of the book catalogue for Baltimore county using external commercial computing facilities. An examination of the various methods (with tables of comparative costs) of producing book catalogues was reported by R M Hayes *and others* ' The economics of book catalog production' *Library resources and technical services* 10 (1) Winter 1966 57-90.

### THE GUARD-BOOK CATALOGUE

In this the entries are made on slips of paper and mounted in the required sequence on the blank leaves of large guard-books. The entries have to be kept as widely spaced as possible to allow for additional insertions and, upon the inevitable filling up of a page, the leaf must be removed, the entries cut up and dispersed over an increased number of leaves.

*Features*: Retains the format of the book catalogue (although it is very much less compact) and permits insertion of entries (albeit with some effort) and updating of the sequence.

*Problems*: The size, number and bulk of the guard-books. The difficulty of maintaining strict order and the length of time taken when cutting up and remounting is required. The constant withdrawals required by most libraries would make this form impracticable for their purposes.

The BM provides a noteworthy example of this form, running to more than twelve hundred volumes (*cf* the printed catalogue in 263 volumes). Some academic libraries still use it.

### THE CARD CATALOGUE

In this each entry is recorded on a separate card of standard size (12·5 cm × 7·5 cm) and the cards are filed in drawers housed in catalogue cabinets.

*Features*: The arrangement permits complete flexibility and maximum ease of insertion of new entries, and withdrawal of others, so that the catalogue can be completely up to date. It has (theoretically) an infinite capability for expansion. It can be fairly easily guided. Cards are reasonably durable and production of entries on them by typewriting or duplication is not unduly expensive. The physical 'spread' of the catalogue (although this can be a problem) permits consultation by many readers at once.

*Problems*: The card form is not thought to be as readily acceptable to all library users as, say, the book form, although the force of this argument has been diminished through the years as the form became widely adopted in libraries. The ability of one reader (in spite of the 'spread' mentioned above) physically to monopolise a whole drawer or section of the cabinet causes problems in busy libraries. The possibility of removal and destruction of the cards (although in most cases they are held by rods) by errant users can create a difficulty. But probably the biggest problem of all, which is increasingly being brought home to the very large libraries, is the sheer bulk and remorseless growth of the card form. While it proves an excellent instrument in respect of a reasonably sized library it can become a massive 'space-eater' in a very large library. A dramatic example of this might be found merely in the title of the following article: F Whitehouse ' NYPL's nightmarish problem: eight million index cards' *Antiquarian bookman* 38 (42) July 1966 4-11.

#### THE SHEAF CATALOGUE
In this each entry is recorded on separate paper slips which are filed in specially made loose-leaf binders.

*Features*: This form is claimed to combine the convenience and 'psychological advantages' of the book-form with the flexibility for insertion and withdrawal of entries of the card catalogue. The entries on paper slips are cheaper to produce than card entries, and can be reproduced cheaply by simple carbon copies. Since slips are usually larger than the standard card more space is available for copy and this has led to their use in regional union catalogues, where the entry has to carry a large grid. It occupies less space than the card cabinets.

*Problems*: While capability for insertion and withdrawal of entries is certainly present, the nature of the binding mechanism on the sheaf holder (screws, springs etc) and the flimsiness of the paper slips make the operations of insertion and withdrawal of entries less convenient. In spite of the 'book form', with one entry per page, 'sequential scanning' is not all that easy, although it may be slightly easier than in the card catalogue. The larger area for the entry gives no distinct advantage unless, as noted above, it is to be used for a grid, or perhaps for annotation. Guiding is not very satisfactory.

Some of the larger libraries in Britain, as well as the regional bureaux, have used and are using sheaf catalogues, but there has never been evidence of distinct advantages of the form over the practically universal card catalogue sufficient to oust the latter from its supremacy.

#### OTHER FORMS
Office equipment manufacturers have, in recent years, produced a wide variety of sophisticated devices for the indexing and

posting of information, which are in direct line of descent from the card file developed for the library catalogue. Visible indexes, whether in the form of narrow strips mounted in a frame, or metal trays holding cards held flat, hinged and so arranged that a projecting edge is available for a heading, provide the same facility for easy interpolation of new entries. D E Davinson *Periodicals: a manual of practice* (London, Deutsch, second edition 1964) pages 59-64 indicates the value of visible indexes for periodicals acquisition. J E Wright ' Rearranging and recataloguing a reference library of books' ASLIB *Proceedings* 2 (1) February 1950 26-32 describes the preparation of a short-title finding list using ' Stripdex '. Their use for the indexing and listing of special categories of material such as gramophone records, illustrations collections etc, where perhaps title entry may be brief but descriptive detail may require the space available on an eight by five or six by four card, is fairly obvious, and many libraries have found that by photocopying the strips or the projecting edges of the visible index cards, they have been able to reproduce usable brief check lists of the materials listed thereon.

READINGS

London University School of Librarianship *Cataloguing principles and practice* edited by Mary Piggott (London, LA, 1954). Chapters 9 and 11 provide, inter alia, information on the employment of the various ' physical forms' in municipal and academic libraries.

Margaret Mann *Introduction to cataloguing and the classification of books* (Chicago, ALA, second edition 1943), chapter 7, section 1 ' The function and form of the catalog' pages 101-103.

C D Needham *Organizing knowledge in libraries* (London, Deutsch, 1964), chapter 17 ' The physical forms of catalogues '.

H A Sharp *Cataloguing: a textbook for use in libraries* (London, Grafton, fourth edition 1948), chapter 14 ' Methods of displaying catalogues '.

M F Tauber *Cataloguing and classification* volume one, part one of *State of the library art* edited by R R Shaw (New Brunswick, Rutgers University Press, 1960). An interesting table of the comparative features of various forms of catalogues by C D Gull is reproduced on pages 69-71, and ' The sheaf catalogue ' is discussed on pages 111-116.

# CHAPTER EIGHT
# CATALOGUING PROCESSES
# AND POLICIES

**W**ITH the commitment of cataloguers to commonly-accepted classification schemes and cataloguing codes, and with their continual and justifiable efforts to attain standardisation in many areas of practice, it may be wondered why so much variation exists in the organisation of cataloguing operations and policies between one library and another. The answer is to be found in the simple fact that a cataloguing department and a cataloguing system, if either is to be efficient and effective, must be designed and operated to answer the specific needs of the library or library system which it serves.

The good management of cataloguing operations requires that many procedures which may be common to all cataloguing operations have to be implemented, not in a vacuum, but in exact relation to a particular library situation. Examples of these procedures are the sorting of material at the pre-cataloguing stage; the question of whether the cataloguing should be divided on a basis of function (*ie* separating or linking descriptive and subject cataloguing, or creating subject specialist cataloguers); the reproduction of cataloguing entries (or the use of printed cards); and many policies are available for adoption, such as analytical cataloguing, selective cataloguing, simplified cataloguing. Obviously, the variety of library situations is very great, and is by no means limited to the differences between, say, academic and public, or special and county, but readily obtains within each group.

The professional cataloguer will develop and operate his system not solely on the basis of what he or she considers to be 'a best way' of doing this or that thing, but on the basis of careful analysis of the library system in respect of such interrelated matters as:

1 The type of library and the purpose it serves.

2 The organisation and disposition of its stock, collections, branches, departments.

3 The nature of its acquisitions.

4 The nature of the library's clientele and the number and types of catalogues which have to be provided for them.

5 The resources in staff and equipment available for cataloguing.

The notes on cataloguing processes and policies given below must be related to these considerations, while the section on cataloguing in different kinds of libraries (page 92 below) should also be read with realisation of the wide differences that can justifiably occur.

## REPRODUCTION OF CATALOGUE ENTRIES

Few technical processes in libraries have produced more invention, adaptation and improvisation than that of catalogue entry reproduction. Ever since it was realised that the same descriptive detail might well be reproduced, on card or sheaf, under a number of different headings in the catalogue, librarians have sought the ideal method of doing this. Individual systems have proliferated in libraries and have been described in library literature, each with its own claim to speed, economy, flexibility or typographical clarity. Some of the very many in general use include:

*The typewriter*: Still the most economical when only two or three cards are required or when, using carbon copies, a small number of sheaf entries are needed.

*The spirit duplicator (hectography)*: An 'art' paper master with a special backing sheet of 'transfer' or carbon paper is used to prepare a typewritten master. The master is then clipped to the duplicator, and by damping copy with spirit as both elements are passed under a rotary drum an image is transferred from master to copy under pressure. *Features*: Economy of materials, speedy processing and drying of copy, 'masking' to give alteration of headings is possible, economic for quite few copies and capable of reproducing 150 or more copies on card before the dye is exhausted. Two particular disadvantages are that the copy is not as 'crisp' as in other methods, and that the image will fade if long exposed to strong sunlight (although there is little danger of this in catalogue files).

*Wax-stencil duplicator*: A wax-stencil master cut by typewriter, fastened round drum containing ink. Ink passes through cut-out stencil to copy under pressure of rotary drum. The copy is very clear, and several thousand copies are possible; reasonably economic in materials used. Disadvantages are the drying time needed for copies (and card stock must be reasonably absorbent), and the fact that no special version of duplicators (with drum-size related to smaller stencil size needed for cards) has been developed yet in the UK.

*Offset lithography*: Provides a number of ways (typing, photography, xerography) of producing the master on a metal or plastic-surfaced mat, employing the lithographic principle of the ink adhering only to the greasy image and being repelled elsewhere on the damped plate. The image is transferred to a rubber blanket and thence to the copy. Excellent, quickly drying copies are obtainable and long runs are possible. But the method is fairly expensive in materials and more so in equipment. Even the smallest offset-litho machine is much more expensive than other types of duplicator and more complex in maintenance.

*Addressing machines*: They may use as masters embossed metal plates, stencils, or hectographic paper, and have the advantage that since they were designed to mechanise the addressing of envelopes, their printing area and ancillary printing equipment approaches that required for standard sizes of catalogue cards. They have proved capable of adaptation for card reproduction, with certain limitations regarding rigidity of layout, number of lines of print available on the master; but a main feature of the addressing machine systems—the ability to store the master indefinitely for continual re-use—provides no essential benefit in most kinds of libraries.

Other copying methods have employed combinations of photographic or xerographic processes, microfilm, multilith, automatic typewriters, and much research and development proceeds. The pamphlet by Philip S Pargeter *The reproduction of catalogue cards* (London, LA 1960) provides basic reading on this subject. The ALA Library Technology Project *Catalogue card reproduction: report on a study conducted by George Fry & Associates* (Chicago, ALA 1965) comprehensively examines and costs some thirteen processes and finds that on a basis of costs, libraries who require cards for 1,000-2,000 titles a year should consider 1 Printed cards, 2 Typing, 3 Reproduction by fluid or stencil duplication. Larger libraries (2,000-9,000 card sets per year) should consider stencil duplication with full-size equipment, offset duplication, and electrostatic copying equipment. An article based on the LTP study is J H Treyz ' Equipment and methods in catalog card reproduction ' *Library resources* 8 (3) Summer 1964 267-278.

The increasing availability of authoritative cataloguing data enshrined in the volumes of the LC catalogues, *National union catalog, British national bibliography* and BM *General catalogue* and many other sources, has led to a search for the 'Cataloguer's camera' which, ideally, would instantly photograph and enlarge entries found in such sources, producing copies on card stock to make sets for insertion in the catalogue. The US Council on Library Resources investigated the production of such a camera shortly after it was set up in 1956, but while some progress was made the camera failed to materialise, apparently on the grounds that perhaps too much was being required of the device *ie* it was required to transfer the tracings at the foot of the LC entries on to the headings of the reproduced cards. However, M Williams ' The CU-5 as a cataloguer's aid ' APLA *Bulletin* 31 (2) May 1967, 53-54 has described the use of a Polaroid close-up camera (originally produced as a dental and medical device) for the transcription of entries from printed sources with the instantly-produced print being used as a workslip for all cataloguing routines, while H Oustinoff ' University of Vermont uses a Polaroid CU-5 to speed book processing' *Library resources and technical services* 11 (4) Fall 1967 474-478 reports that the same device has been used in her library since 1965. An accompanying article in this same issue of *LRTS*, M H Stranger ' The cataloguer's camera ' described a similar approach using a less portable device in use in Indiana University.

CENTRAL CATALOGUING AGENCIES AND THE USE OF PRINTED CARDS
No one is more conscious of the duplication of effort and wasteful repetition than the cataloguer establishing the entry for a new, and perhaps difficult book, who knows that hundreds of other cataloguers, using the same codes and classification schedules, are probably doing precisely the same thing at approximately the same time. This is a paradoxical situation which can be avoided by the creation of a central authority where the opera-

tion of classifying and cataloguing of books can be done, and the entries then made available to libraries throughout the country.

The Library of Congress, as a by-product of cataloguing its acquisitions, has made copies of its printed cards available for purchase and use by libraries since 1901. The cards carry LC and DC class numbers, subject heading tracings, and an LC serial number. The serial numbers are carried in the US trade bibliographies—Wilson's *Cumulative book index,* Bowker's *Publisher's weekly* and *Book publishing record,* and using these numbers US librarians can order card sets from LC at the same time as they order the titles from the bookseller.

The UK had to wait until 1950 to see the beginnings of a similar central service. The British National Bibliography, working from the books received by legal deposit in the British Museum, produces a weekly printed list with entries classified and arranged by 14th and 16th editions of DC (with BNB notational modifications) and with author/title index. A subject index on the chain principle is provided in the last issue of each month. There are quarterly, half-yearly, nine-monthly, annual and five-yearly cumulations. A printed card service was commenced in 1956, and for material recorded from the first of January that year, cards could be purchased from BNB, using the BNB serial number cited in the entry. The cards carry the ' BNB version of DC ' as class marks, and have detailed feature headings most suitable for classified catalogues, but giving some guidance for alphabetical subject heading work. Certain categories of material are omitted, *eg* maps, some government publications such as parliamentary papers, cheap novelettes, reprints etc. BNB found it necessary in 1962 to exclude US publications issued through UK outlets. (It should be noted that LC cards, since they represent the library's acquisitions, cover much foreign material, while BNB cards are essentially a by-product of a national bibliography.) A J Wells has described the card service in ' Printed catalogue cards ' *Journal of documentation* 13 (2) 1957 67-71.

The BNB from its inception has displayed a remarkable capacity for making quite sweeping changes in some of its practices, a capacity which might not be expected to be found in a body committed to producing a national bibliographical service and a national cataloguing service. Some examples of this are to be found in its switch from orthodox DC numbers to applying ' verbal extensions' after the arbitrary sign ' [1] ' in 1951, and later again, in 1960, grafting an alpha-numerical supplementary notation onto DC numbers, to achieve more exact subject specification by means of this classification. Such changes were not greeted always with universal applause by BNB users.

Among changes put into operation at the beginning of 1968 have been: the laudable adoption of the *Anglo-American cataloguing rules, 1967;* a newly designed entry with a better typeface which produces a more legible entry in both printed booklist and card; a DC number printed at the foot of those entries bearing the BNB ' supplementary notation ' number. (It is further indicated that attention is being given to placing a current official DC number on *every* entry—it might be wondered why this was not done years ago.) Tracings, in accordance with AACR recommendations, will be given at the foot of the entry on the weekly list. Coverage will be extended to include fiction reprints in paperback and non-governmental Irish Republic books, both excluded in 1962. But, tracings will *not* be given on printed cards, nor will they, or the more orthodox DC number, be entered in the quarterly, annual, and other cumulations. The justification of this is thus stated, ' It is intended for reasons of economy and space to develop the weekly lists as a cataloguing tool and to concentrate on providing a bibliographical service only in the cumulations '. If such a decision persists, as time goes by, cataloguers searching long files of weekly issues for full cataloguing data, instead of being able to refer to the handier cumulations, may find BNB's use of the word ' economy ' singularly inappropriate to their own situation.

BNB is presently entering the ' standard book number ' (SBN) in the imprint section of the entry, immediately after date of publication. This individualising identification number for (at present) British, American and Australian books, which encodes the publisher, title, volume or edition, and a check digit in a number suitable for computer usage is described in ' Standard book numbering: why it is needed and how it will function ' *The Bookseller* 3205 May 27 1967 2352-2364. A decision to abandon the BNB serial number in favour of the SBN was postponed because of the difficulty which ' such abandonment might create in certain library processes ' (*Liaison* October 1967 p78).

For good or ill, the BNB all too often has not shown much consideration for its users, and indeed, precise information relating to its usage has emerged only lately as a result of a research project. P R Lewis ' BNB printed cards: distribution and use in British libraries' *Catalogue and index* (8) October 1967 8-10 *and* ' British National Bibliography provision in public libraries' *Library Association record* 70 (1) Jan 1968 14-16, reports on a research programme carried out with the support of the Council of the BNB, finding that of 303 purchasers of printed cards in 1966, sixty per cent were public libraries, while national and university libraries only accounted for some three per cent of card sales. With regard to book list subscriptions, public libraries are the major users once again, taking some sixty one per cent of the subscriptions.

Use of BNB in cataloguing may range from total acceptance of its services, using the weekly list as the book-selection and book-ordering instrument (at the same time ordering the relevant printed cards or sheafs, or transcribing the relevant entries, and adding required headings) to more limited use as a guide to establishing headings and some descriptive details, for incorporation into the library's chosen form of entry. The use of BNB in a library system was described by S F Harper ' BNB cards at Willesden' *Library Association record* 59 (8) August 1957 269-271. G Walters 'Cataloguing in the Department of Printed Books' *Library Association record* 65 (4) April 1963 151-155 tells of BNB use in the National Library of Wales. L M Cowburn ' BNB cards in City University' *Catalogue & index* (10) April 1968 8-10 describes the adoption of printed cards at the new university, emphasising the need for acceptance of standardisation of practice in cataloguing before engaging in the 'current rush to the computer'.

The production of machine-readable catalogue data by BNB on lines similar to the LC ' Project MARC' (see chapter nine) is foreshadowed in two papers by the editor A J Wells, ' The *British national bibliography*' *Brasenose conference on the automation of libraries* (London, Mansell 1967) pp 24-32 and ' Role of the *British national bibliography* in the application of computers to public library systems' ASLIB *Proceedings* (18) September 1966 263-7.

*Cataloguing-in-source*: To have every published book bearing on the verso of its title-page an authoritative catalogue entry and tracings may be something of a cataloguer's dream, but cataloguing-in-source (or what Ranganathan has called 'pre-natal' cataloguing) was the subject of a notable experiment by LC cataloguers aided by a grant from the Council on Library Resources. Cataloguers worked from advance proof-sheets and from bibliographical information supplied by the publishers before publication. The cataloguers found the data difficult to handle in form and content, only about half of the 300 publishers invited co-operated and there were many complaints of inconvenience and disruption of schedules. It was found that LC would need more money, more staff and at least three regional centres to operate the system properly, and the rather disappointing conclusion of the Library of Congress *The cataloguing-in-source experiment: a report* (Washington, LC, 1960) was that the programme 'could not be justified from the viewpoint of financing, technical considerations, or utility.' Comprehensive reviews of the report appeared in *Library resources* 4 (4) 1960 269-284.

The abandonment, justifiable or otherwise, of this particular experiment, provides no evidence of lack of need for centralised cataloguing. As cataloguing and book processing costs increase, there is an ever-increasing awareness of the logic of achieving economies of scale, and elimination of the wasteful duplication of human effort, by setting up area and regional processing centres to serve groups of libraries from a central source. This development is most evident in the United States where co-operative state, and regional, processing centres have emerged in unprecedented numbers in recent years.

*Shared cataloguing*: One of the most dramatic and far-reaching developments in centralised cataloguing was briefly and quietly announced in 'Report on a conference on shared cataloguing, London, January 13, 1966' *Library of Congress information bulletin* 25 (7) February 1966 *appendix*. Representatives of LC, BM, BNB, Bibliothèque Nationale and several other European national libraries had agreed that LC should receive for cataloguing purposes the entries in the various national bibliographies, securing a copy of the listings as soon as possible, even in advance of the publication of the national bibliography.

Behind this agreement lay the work of many American librarians, not least that of the Shared Cataloguing Committee of the American Association of Research Libraries. Set up in 1963 to consider the problem that almost half the acquisitions in the major US libraries were not covered by LC printed cards, the committee decided that the answer was not to be found in co-operative cataloguing but in *centralised cataloguing* with Library of Congress as the central source. The representatives of the committee, supported by other library organisations and the Library of Congress, succeeded in having Title II-C written into the US Higher Education Act of 1965 whereby (NPAC) the National Program for Acquisitions and Cataloguing, otherwise known as the 'Shared Cataloguing Program', came into being. Title II-C authorises the Library of Congress to become globally comprehensive in its acquisitions of scholarly materials, and to provide cataloguing data for such acquisitions *promptly* after receipt, distributing such data by printed cards and by any other means.

With the necessary funds available, LC acted swiftly in response to its widened role and responsibilities. In June 1967 there were Shared Cataloguing Offices in most of the principal cities in Europe, one in South America and one in Africa and more to come. These offices, working in conjunction with the national sources of bibliographic data, acquire the descriptive copy of catalogue entries as soon as possible, carry out preliminary conversion work so that the entry will conform in heading and some other details with LC practice, select and acquire the appropriate books and ship books and cards by air to the Shared Cataloging Division at LC. LC accept as much as possible of the original entry, adding such details as LC and DC class numbers and LC subject headings, and publishes the final printed card entry as rapidly as it can.

To the cataloguers and subject bibliographers who are aware of the painfully slow and almost reluctant acceptance of the ancient and historic arguments for centralised bibliographic control in the quite modest local or national contexts, the swift and near-effortless emergence of LC as the international centre for the collection, formulation and distribution of bibliographical information and cataloguing data may seem almost miraculous. Representing as it does the agreement of so many librarians, libraries and agencies on an international basis and linked with the possibility of interchange of the cataloguing information by means of newer media (see chapter nine), shared cataloguing offers immediate benefits of international library co-operation in the vital area of cataloguing. Papers given at the 33rd session of the IFLA General Council, Toronto, August 1967 and published in *Libri* 17 (4) 1967 270-304 give a most complete account of the Shared Cataloguing Program. In particular, J E Skipper 'International implications of the Shared Cataloguing Program: introductory statement pp 270-275 'gives an historical account of the development of the idea, while J G Lorenz 'International implications of the Shared Cataloging Program: planning for bibliographic control' pp 276-284 describes in some detail the operations at both the Library of Congress and the offices abroad. Other accounts are available in J W Cronin *and others* 'Centralized cataloguing at the national and international level ' *Library resources and technical services* 11 (1) Winter 1967 27-29 and H M Welch 'Implications for resources and technical services' (in 'The Higher Education Act of 1965: a symposium') *College and research libraries* 27 (5) September 1966 340-345.

SIMPLIFIED AND SELECTIVE CATALOGUING

A cataloguing code will prescribe the amount of descriptive detail to be recorded in respect of a book or document and, in appropriate cases, indicate which added entries should be made under other headings. But the codes cannot consider such factors as the relative importance in a particular library of a two-page document and a scholarly treatise, between ephemeral material which will quickly go out of date and soon be discarded, and other material considered to be of permanent value. Librarians, however, faced with the continuing high cost of cataloguing and with the not infrequent situation of an ever-increasing volume of acquisitions outstripping the capability of cataloguers to deal with it, have sometimes sought an answer to these problems in the policies of simplified cataloguing and/or selective cataloguing.

*Simplified cataloguing* is limiting the *amount of descriptive detail* recorded in the entry. It may range from a modest decision to reduce the full collation statement as prescribed in the code, to a drastic reduction of entry to a form just barely capable of identifying the book or document (*eg* author's surname with initials, short title, edition, date). The policy of simplified cataloguing (depending on the amount of 'simplification' and the nature of the library) may be applied to all descriptive practice, or may be restricted to certain kinds of materials, ephemera, pamphlets and brochures; or to fiction and children's books in a public library.

*Selective cataloguing* means limiting the *number of entries* in respect of different kinds of material entering the library. Again, depending upon the nature of the library, it might be determined that certain materials such as reference and research works require full cataloguing with all possible added entries, while what is considered to be more 'transient' material will not receive added entries. Other material consisting of groups of documents (HMSO, UN, UNESCO) may be considered to be 'self-indexing', especially if the collection is fairly comprehensive and a marked-up checklist or printed catalogue is separately available. It may be decided that it is sufficient to refer under appropriate headings in the catalogue to the existence of separate document collections and lists.

In support of such policies it can be said that the range of materials acquired in most libraries and the varying values thereof, often seem to indicate the necessity for differential treatment; and again, any policy which tends to speed the process of cataloguing and thus makes material, to whatever extent, more quickly available, seems desirable. However, this has to be balanced against the possibility that a cataloguing system which creates differential treatments in the work-flow can be uneconomic also. For example, sorting the books and documents into categories can be time-consuming, and applying different rules to different categories may be equally as expensive as applying uniform treatment to all material. There is the added danger that by simplifying too much, some bibliographical work may be removed from the shoulders of the cataloguers, simply to be placed on those of other library staff.

The Library of Congress policy of 'limited cataloguing' which has been frequently cited as an example of simplified cataloguing in action, included a division of books and documents into four categories, each receiving differential treatment according to the rules given in *Cataloguing rules . . . additions and changes* (1949-58) pages 73-76. F Bernice Field, chairman of the ALA Descriptive Cataloguing Committee, briefly reported on the cessation of the

89

policy in August 1963 in *Library resources* 8 (3) Summer 1964 301 stating simply that 'A study of their experience of eleven years with the rules and of comments received from card subscribers and others led them to the conclusion that a single set of rules should be in force for all publications'. An interesting account of fairly extreme simplified *and* selective cataloguing is described in R K Engelbarts and H D Williams ' Brieflisting: a method for controlling catalogue arrears ' *Library resources* 9 (2) Spring 1965 191-199 whereby some 60,000 backlog items had *one* card bearing author's name, shelf number and reduced photofacsimile of the title page inserted in the catalogue. D Benson ' Instant cataloguing ' *Canadian library* 22 (6) May 1966 419-421 describes a one-entry system with simplified title-page-available data transcribed by non-professional cataloguers, headings being taken from LC catalogues and other sources, employed in the National Library of Canada for several hundred thousand uncatalogued items.

ANALYTICAL CATALOGUING

Analytical entries can be made for individual parts of a book or document under author or subject or title of the part analysed, and may be made sometimes under all three headings. Analytical cataloguing is frequently necessary in the case of composite works and collections (*eg* a catalogue listing an entry under editor heading for a collection entitled ' Six one-act plays ' is obviously less effective than if it contains author and title analyticals for each of the plays as well) but the extent to which such analysis of the contents of anthologies, collections (literary, biographical etc), periodical publications, proceedings, symposia *can* be carried out is obviously conditioned by the particular library situation and the amount of extra work involved, not to mention the possible additional bulk of entries added to the catalogue.

Such analytical cataloguing tends to be restricted to: 1 the special library where the greatest depth of subject analysis of a relatively small stock is required for the specialist user; 2 special subject collections or local history collections in the general library where, again, it is desirable, and perhaps possible, to probe into the contents of works to make the maximum amount of information available.

Such analysis presumes the unavailability or prohibitive cost of published bibliographical services and indexes. In a sizable general library, analytical cataloguing on a large scale is impracticable, but the provision of a comprehensive bibliographical collection can offer a substantial solution in providing (by means of periodical indexing services and current subject bibliographies) much analysis of library holdings not analysed in the catalogue, and in giving the library an extra capability to make bibliographical searches beyond the mere limits of its own catalogue. There has been a continuing debate on the exact relationship that should obtain between the library catalogue and the published bibliographical services, in respect of the analytical cataloguing and indexing function (*cf* R C Swank 'Subject catalogs, classifications, or bibliographies?' *Library quarterly* 14 October 1944 316-322), but the growth in number of such services seems to indicate that more and more analytical work is being transferred to them. A recent investigation in Germany into analytical cataloguing, reported by O Löhmann 'The subject-cataloguing of the contents of periodicals as a task of comprehensive libraries' *Libri* 17 (2) 1967 95-103 came to the conclusion that although analytical cataloguing of all periodicals was desirable, practicality would indicate its limitation to such items as 'progress reports in various subject areas', linking this work with an improvement in the provision of bibliographies in the libraries.

ANNOTATION

The catalogue 'note' which may give necessary additional information concerning title, edition, imprint or collation, or which sets forth a list of contents, still comes within the realm of orthodox descriptive cataloguing. Any additional note which may purport to give information concerning the intellectual content of the work, whether purely informative, or critical and evaluative, is considered to be an annotation.

Annotations on entries, if made at all (and the practice has declined in most library catalogues since the more stately days when there was a gentle flow of acquisitions and unhurried cataloguers), must necessarily be limited in length, about thirty words being generally considered acceptable. Most desirably, they should concentrate on the factual, giving such details as 1 author's status or authority in relation to his subject; 2 the level of treatment; 3 the type of reader at whom the work is aimed. Critical or evaluative annotations which would present the reader with the cataloguer's assessment of the importance, value and merit of the work are usually to be avoided, if only for the obvious reason that, unless the cataloguer is a subject specialist, such judgements can hardly be valid. (One method of overcoming the latter difficulty is sometimes to be found in the use of quotations from authoritative reviews, but even this method, as in publishers' blurbs, can result in bias.)

Annotations nowadays are perhaps most useful and most valid when used in subject booklists and reading lists aimed at creating interest in a special subject, or designed for a special group of readers such as children; but even here, any annotation which overruns the purely informative probably should be left to the subject specialists. A survey of catalogue annotation was reported by P Ward 'Annotation in public library catalogues: British practice and policy', *Library Association record* 64 (6) June 1962 208-212.

The LC printed cards for children's literature, the issue of which began in 1966, carry a brief annotation, descriptive of the content, located just below the imprint and above the cataloguing note (if any). The mixed reception given to this card service was not focused on the annotation but on the differentials inserted in subject heading practice and added entry specification, *see* ' Crisis or cul-de-sac' *Library journal* 91 (18) October 15 1966 5129-5132.

CATALOGUING IN DIFFERENT KINDS OF LIBRARIES
*Municipal libraries*: These may vary in size from a single library building to a complex system of central library with subject departments, branch libraries and smaller centres. Acquisitions will be largely of current material. The clientèle will range from children beginning to read to scholars doing research in the reference library. Full catalogues will usually be required at all major service points, and a central master catalogue is necessary in a big system.

Practices may include the use of printed cards, (forty per cent of the public libraries replying to the LA Library Research Committee BNB questionnaire reported that they did so, see *Library Association record* 67 (2) February 1965 52 and the survey by P R

Lewis (see p 85) has shown that forty per cent of UK public libraries purchase eighty per cent of the BNB printed cards).

Printed cards involve a sorting of acquisitions into BNB and non-BNB, the latter being catalogued to a similar standard. The establishment of a central cataloguing department is widely accepted as the most efficient approach, and the general tendency would appear to be against dividing the cataloguing work functionally or by subject, although the subject division approach at Tottenham in North London should be noted. (A W McClellan ' Organization of a public library for subject specialization' *Library Association record* 57 (8) August 1955 296-303.)

Selective cataloguing may be applied to ephemeral material and document collections. Simplified cataloguing may be applied to children's library catalogues. Analytical cataloguing, except for local history and special subject collections, is rarely possible. Annotation will usually be confined to book lists.

The merger of many previously separate London library authorities as a result of the reorganisation of the London boroughs in 1965 threw much light on the differing methods and approaches to classification and catalogue provision employed therein. W S H Ashmore ' Cataloguing, classification and book provision in the new London boroughs' *Assistant librarian* 59 (4) April 1966 74-77 discusses the problems of classification and cataloguing in the amalgamation of systems which had previously used various editions of DC and the Brown ' Subject classification ', and employed both classified and dictionary forms of catalogue. He considers that the best hope for the problems of these larger bibliographic service areas may lie in computerised catalogue systems. F Bennett ' Mergers and catalogues' *Library Association record* 70 (4) April 1968 100-102 describes the integration of three separate cataloguing systems in the new London Borough of Tower Hamlets, finding it necessary to carry out conversion operations in a more conventional manner before computerisation can be considered.

*County libraries*: The features usually include a headquarters building, with a large central collection, controlling a widely scattered array of branches (full-time and part-time), library centres and mobiles. The stock and clientèle are essentially the same as in the municipal libraries but, unlike the cities and towns with concentrated populations, where the readers reasonably can be expected to travel to the static service points, the problem in the counties is to get the books to the readers by providing a greater number of widely-spaced and necessarily smaller service points and mobile libraries.

A central union catalogue of holdings and a centralised cataloguing department is essential. While full catalogues may be necessary at the larger branches, they cannot easily be provided at the smaller centres with stock constantly changing, and thus book-lists and lists of current acquisitions are of great importance. The removal of branch catalogues and substitution of a teleprinter at each branch to link with the headquarters catalogue is an interesting development in Buckinghamshire (G Jones 'From book box to telex: mechanization for county libraries' LA *Conference papers,* 1962, pages 90-101).

*University libraries*: The features may include a main library with a number of special collections, some branch libraries which are essentially subject libraries (medicine, science etc) and a number of departmental libraries ranging from collections of several thousand volumes down to a few hundred. Acquisitions will include a very high proportion of pre-current material, reprints, and foreign imprints. The readership will range from undergraduates requiring material for their courses to postgraduates doing highly specialised research. A central master catalogue of all works is essential in the main library, and branch libraries require catalogues of holdings, but the provision of detailed catalogues in the departmental locations is rarely considered essential.

In the UK, few university libraries use printed cards (perhaps three or four out of about fifty libraries), this being in part due to the nature of their acquisitions. Emphasis may be on a scholarly author/title catalogue (with little or no selective cataloguing), and there may be a consequent tendency to make lesser provision for the subject approach. (US university libraries, however, make much use of LC cards, and there is no neglect of the subject catalogue.) The sorting of acquisitions, and the division of the cataloguing operations, may be on a subject basis. Annotation is rarely possible, while the size of the collections excludes the possibility of much analytical cataloguing and requires dependence on published indexes and bibliographical services.

J Friedman and A Jeffreys 'Cataloguing and classification in British university libraries; a survey of practices and procedures' *Journal of documentation* 23 (3) September 1967 179-272 (also separately published by Sheffield University Postgraduate School of Librarianship, 1967) report in detail and depth on practice in fifty one libraries which returned an elaborate questionnaire. The general picture emerging is, not unexpectedly, one of great diversity. LC classification is the most widely used, AA rules are most widely accepted (but modifications on any classification schemes and cataloguing codes used, are extensively made). The ' author' catalogue is usually a ' name' catalogue, but one quarter of the libraries have no subject catalogues (those that have, favour the classified form). Little use is made of printed cards or centralised services. Wide differences in most matters of cataloguing practice and detail obtain. Reading the results of this survey, it is difficult to escape the conclusion that the cataloguers in most British academic libraries have not felt themselves to be affected by many matters which, for so long, have been the concern of most other cataloguers—rationalisation of practice being only one example.

*Special libraries*: The library must be directed not so much to the provision of books and documents as to providing an information service derived from them. Acquisitions may include a relatively small proportion of books and a high proportion of periodicals, abstracting literature, report literature. The clientèle will be specialists in the subject field of the library.

The catalogue of the bookstock may be conventional, but much analytical cataloguing of both books and periodicals may be required, with great emphasis on the subject approach, and the provision of abstracts. Selective cataloguing may be used for transient material such as trade catalogues. More and more special libraries inundated with 'report literature' are using 'unconventional' methods (*ie* co-ordinate indexing) allied with mechanical sorting, to retrieve information from such document collections. B R F Kyle in 'Notes on cataloguing in special libraries with special emphasis on author and name entries' *Journal of documentation* 22 (1) March 1966 13-21 points out that special library catalogues must be primarily finding tools, and entries (which may be multiple entries on unit cards), should be evaluated in this light.

Four chapters in pages 93-144 of the London University School of Librarianship publication *Cataloguing principles and practice* edited by Mary Piggott give useful accounts of practice in the various types of libraries (chapter 9, S J Butcher ' Municipal libraries '; chapter 10, L Paulin ' County libraries '; chapter 11, R S Mortimer ' University libraries '; chapter 12 L Jolley ' Special libraries '). M Piggott ' Cataloguing practice in university and special libraries ' *Library Association record* 56 (5) May 1954 160-166 and B A Custer ' Some unanswered questions: the public library ' *Library quarterly* 26 (4) October 1956 356-361, both deal with cataloguing problems in these types of library. The chapter by J R Sharp on ' Information retrieval ' in W Ashworth ed *Handbook of special librarianship and information work* (London, ASLIB third edition 1967) pages 141-232 not only provides a comprehensive account of special library cataloguing and indexing, but ranges widely over the field of cataloguing; codes, entry, forms of catalogues, subject cataloguing theory and practice, and provides useful reading on these matters.

READINGS

Margaret Mann *Introduction to cataloguing and the classification of books* (Chicago, ALA, second edition 1943). Chapter 17 ' Organization and administration of the catalog department ' and pages 153-154 ' Subject analyticals '.

C D Needham *Organizing knowledge in libraries* (London, Deutsch 1964). Chapter 18 ' Centralized cataloguing '; chapter 20 ' Process of cataloguing '; chapter 14 ' Analytical cataloguing '; pages 169-173 'Annotation '.

D M Norris *A primer of cataloguing* (London, AAL, 1952). Chapter 11 ' Simplified and selective cataloguing '.

H A Sharp *Cataloguing: a textbook for use in libraries* (London, Grafton fourth edition 1948). Chapter 10 'Annotation '.

A H Trotier ' The organization and administration of cataloging processes ' *Library trends* 2 (2) October 1953 264-278.

# CHAPTER NINE: CATALOGUING AND INFORMATION RETRIEVAL METHODS

THE present relationship of cataloguing to information storage and retrieval—of the 'classifiers' to the 'mechanicals', of the 'conventional cataloguers' to the 'information indexers'—might be described with some reservations as tending towards recognition that both practices, and both practitioners, have much more in common than most of the literature relating to their development over the past two decades might suggest.

Even if it is difficult to grasp the implications of some of the sweeping statements which have been made—*eg*, that half of all the scientific research ever done has been done since 1950—there can be no disputing the fact that the vast expansion of scientific and technical research in recent years has produced what has been called 'the information explosion'; and, due to the volume and complexity of the information produced, a crisis in communication of scientific and technical data between persons and between institutions working in the field of science and technology. The 'paper explosion' which has been a direct consequence of this can scarcely be measured. Estimates of the number of scientific and technical periodicals published annually have not been lower than 30,000 (carrying between one and two million articles annually), and the amount of information enshrined in the research 'report literature' cannot begin to be assessed.

To attempt to meet this problem, to organise on behalf of the technologies, industries and sciences, a means of storing information (not merely documents) and of retrieving the relevant and the required, there emerged a new group of workers, technically-trained and scientifically orientated. These people, even when organising document collections and recorded scientific knowledge for purposeful use, were most often unaware that their activities to any extent paralleled those of librarians and cataloguers; or, if they were conscious of a parallel, they tended to reject it. They brought to bear on the problem of technical documentation the 'analytical scientific approach' (with a consequent development of specialised, and frequently esoteric terminology) and they sought, whenever possible and with varying degrees of success, to substitute mechanical and technical equipment for the manual 'conventional' methods.

Calvin Mooers, who has made many contributions to the terminology, 'zatocoding', 'descriptor', etc, first used the term 'information retrieval' in 1950, and under this heading a vast and imposing literature describing theories, methods and systems has developed and continues to grow. Much of it is repetitive and redundant, much of it is slight and unimportant, much of it shows clear indications that many of the authors are 're-inventing the wheel' every so often—rediscovering an already known system or describing the slightest of variations upon it. But, when this has been said, it must be allowed that information storage and retrieval workers have made important and original advances in their field and in the development of indexing theory and practice. They have contributed much that is relevant and important to the conventional cataloguer and indexer.

CO-ORDINATE INDEXING—UNITERMS

Dr Mortimer Taube 'Uniterms in co-ordinate indexing' *American documentation* 3 (4) October 1952 213-218, and *Studies in co-ordinate indexing* volume one (Washington, Documentation Inc, 1953), developed the uniterm indexing system in the early fifties as a means of dealing with the mass of research reports, derived from scientific research projects, pouring into the US Armed Services Technical Information Agency (ASTIA) at that time.

The system makes no attempt to impose subject arrangement on the documents, each being given a simple serial (or accession) number, and filed in sequence. As originally proposed, the indexer freely extracts from the words in the title, abstract, or text, a list of those words which are considered indicative of the subject content. Relationship and sequence of one term to another is ignored, and all chosen terms are treated as having equal value and are established as separate headings or 'unit terms' on the entries in the index. Each 'term' card will carry, in a pattern made more orderly by the employment of numbered columns, a display of the numbers of all documents for which the index term has been chosen. Thus, for example, document 66 on the subject of 'Building in India in the twelfth century' will have perhaps separate uniterm entries for 'India', for 'building', for 'twelfth century', each entry bearing the number 66. Using the index then involves the searcher in selecting the descriptive terms for his subject, removing the appropriate term cards and scanning them for a common number. The term cards are co-ordinates in the system, and the location of sought documents is indicated at 'the intersection of the co-ordinates', being the number or numbers found common to all of them.

Amongst the advantages claimed for the method are: 1 the speed of filing the document (no need to assign a complex classification notation); 2 faster indexing, with indexer using terms available in title and text; 3 faster searching since each term entry carries *all* relevant numbers on the one term card, unlike the more conventional catalogue 'item entry' with one document description per card; 4 facility with which the system can be used by mechanical indexing methods (see below, page 102).

Criticisms include: 1 accession number order of documents means approach must *always* be made in the index, direct access to the document collection not being possible; 2 the 'simplicity' of using 'title-available' language is more apparent than real, *ie* ambiguity of terms, synonyms, generic to specific relationships, create real difficulties; 3 a high percentage of 'false drops' can occur, *ie* the use of hypothetical uniterms cited above might not yield documents on 'Building in India in the twelfth century', but perhaps 'twelfth century buildings in India'.

These last two difficulties have led later developments and modifications in co-ordinate indexing towards the production of dictionaries of 'controlled uniterms', or 'thesauri of descriptors' which simply represent a move towards establishing an accepted and agreed vocabulary for the indexer (and the searcher). This strongly reflects the conventional alphabetical subject catalogue's progression from subject 'catchword' entry derived from title to the use of established lists of subject headings.

Since 1952 there has been widespread interest and much experimentation in co-ordinate indexing method and the term entry. Application in a wide variety of document collections, using an extensive array of manual and mechanical methods and equipment, has been reported in innumerable articles. A recent account, which includes discussion on the pros and cons of the system, is to be found in J C Costello *Co-ordinate indexing* (New Brunswick, Rutgers University Press 1966). L Jolley has discussed the method in 'The mechanics of co-ordinate indexing' ASLIB *Proceedings* 15 (6) June 1963 161-169.

OTHER INFORMATION RETRIEVAL SYSTEMS

C P Bourne, *Methods of information handling* (New York, Wiley 1963) chapter two, comments upon the wide variety of approaches to information indexing and admits that 'no real fundamental differences could be found among many techniques examined... in many cases it was extremely difficult to determine the precise differences between subject headings, descriptors, uniterms etc.' Nevertheless, accepting an approach suggested by Vickery, he arranges 'documentation schools' or methods according to the 'increasing degree of control exercised on the growth and use of the indexing language'.

The *first* group, covering methods which rely on choosing words from text, contains among others 'Co-ordinate uniterm system' already described, as well as 'keyword-in-context indexing' (KWIC), which is a method of selecting keywords in a document title and printing them with some of the preceding and some of the following words to show the context of the keyword. KWIC can be done manually or by computer, but its subject indexing power, being confined to title words, however permuted, has its limitations. H P Luhn has described the system in 'Keyword-in-context index for technical literature' *American documentation* 11 (4) October 1960 288-295.

The *second* group covers the methods which propose assigning entries from fixed authority lists or classification schemes and, in addition to 'conventional cataloguing and classification', would include Calvin Mooers Descriptor system. His Descriptor is a broad heading that stands for an idea or concept, but is most carefully chosen to suit the needs of the particular group of index users and is thus tailored precisely to their search vocabulary. Mooers describes the basis of his Descriptors and how they are chosen in a paper 'The indexing language of an information retrieval system' in W Simonton *(ed) Information retrieval today*

(Minneapolis, University of Minnesota, 1963) pages 21-36, asserting that the list of thesaurus of Descriptors for any chosen subject field should not exceed two hundred and fifty.

Bourne's *third* group covers 'assignment of entries from authority lists or classification schemes representative of several viewpoints or aspects of subject' and includes UDC, Ranganathan's colon classification, chain-indexing, the recent work of the Classification Research Group in England on faceted classification, and the work on the 'semantic code' developed by J W Perry, A Kent and others at Western Reserve University. This has been described by B C Vickery 'The structure of semantic coding: a review' *American documentation* 10 (3) July 1959 234-241.

Chapter three, pages 43-68 of J Becker and R M Hayes *Information storage and retrieval* (New York, Wiley 1963) covers the same ground as Bourne's work, uses much the same grouping of 'schools' and is a comparative reading.

THE CRANFIELD PROJECT
An important comparative testing of some of the systems of subject cataloguing and information retrieval was carried out at the College of Aeronautics at Cranfield, in Bedfordshire, UK. The project was directed by C W Cleverdon for ASLIB and financed by the National Science Foundation. The four systems tested were: 1 alphabetical subject catalogue, using a subject headings list: 2 UDC classified catalogue with an alphabetical index to UDC numbers; 3 classified catalogue arranged by a specially constructed faceted scheme with a chain index; 4 a uniterm co-ordinate index using an 'authority' list of uniterms. As well as the system, such variables as the indexer, the indexer's rate of learning and the indexing time were tested. The work of indexing 18,000 documents (half in the field of high-speed aerodynamics, half in the general field of aeronautics) by the four systems took three indexers two years. Some 1,200 ' test questions ' were put to each of the four systems and the results statistically analysed.

C W Cleverdon's *Report on the first stage of an investigation into the comparative efficiency of indexing systems* (College of Aerodynamics, Cranfield 1960) and *Report on the testing and analysis of an investigation* (1962) provide the basis for the excellent account given by B C Vickery *On retrieval system theory* (London, Butterworths second edition 1965) pages 168-177. Vickery tabulates the conclusions concisely on pages 170-171. Some of the findings indicated that: 1 the recall ratio (percentage of sought documents successfully retrieved) of all four systems was very close (although the chain index on the faceted system had to be modified to bring it up to a level comparable with the others); 2 ' there was no significant difference in the case of retrieving items indexed by different indexers '; 3 increased time spent on indexing improved the chance of recall; 4 faulty indexing caused sixty per cent of the failures to retrieve source documents (the others being caused by question failures (seventeen per cent), searching failures (seventeen per cent), system failures (six per cent)).

In the light of the project's failure to provide a clear answer to the basic question of which system *was* the most effective, a second ASLIB-Cranfield project was mounted, confining itself to studying *the methods* which might be employed to test the efficiency of various retrieval systems. The first report of Cranfield II is contained in C W Cleverdon *and others Factors determining the performance of indexing systems, Vol 1: Design* (Cranfield, 1966).

MANUAL, MECHANICAL, ELECTRONIC EQUIPMENT

Most of the information retrieval systems are so intimately linked with the use of specialised sorting and filing equipment that in many systems described it is difficult if not impossible to decide which element contributes most to the claimed advantages—the inherent virtues of the indexing methods, or the mechanical capability of the devices used. Whether the item entry or term entry approach is employed, a considerable array of filing and sorting mechanisms are available. They include:

*Visual*: 1 the conventional catalogue card or sheaf (item entry); 2 the uniterm card ruled in columns for posting the document numbers (term entry); 3 the optical stencil or ' peek-a-boo ' card which is centre punched, each punch-hole usually representing a document number as in the uniterm card. The cards bearing the term headings are selected and compared by observing the points at which light passes through, these coordinate points representing the numbers of the sought documents (term entry).

*Manual*: edge-notched (or marginal punched) cards, usually used for item entry, with holes indicating coding positions located on the edges of the card. Coding is done by punching open the appropriate positions on the edges. Searching is done by inserting needles into the pack at the required code positions, lifting it, and thus causing the sought cards to drop.

*Mechanical*: machine sorted punched cards, which are available in a number of sizes up to the limit of eighty columns and 960 punch positions. They may be used for item or term entry but require much ancillary equipment for punching, sorting, collation.

*Electronic*: the computer, which at present represents the ultimate in filing, sorting, storing and printing-out capability. Input may be through the media of punched cards or paper-tape; storage on magnetic core, tape or disc; output via a high-speed line printer (from five hundred up to five thousand lines a minute). The capability of the computer to deal with information retrieval systems, and indeed with conventional cataloguing systems, has been adequately demonstrated in numerous articles, and in indexes and catalogues already produced.

*Microform devices*: the possibility of storing in the searching device not merely a code number, a descriptive entry, or an abstract, but an actual copy of the required text in microform, has led to the development of electronic equipment which can scan reels of microfilm at high speed and photocopy 'on the run' the required frames in response to a coding system located alongside the micro-image. R R Shaw's 'rapid selector' and its successor FLIP both use this principle, which, it should be noted, requires the whole file to be searched each time. A microfilm has been built into the machine-sorted punched card to make the 'aperture card' which can be retrieved by mechanical sorting. 'Minicards' (about half the size of a postage stamp) have been developed and provide records which will carry both micro-image and a coding system which responds to a photo-selection device.

John R Sharp 'Advantages of non-conventional systems' chapter five of *Some fundamentals of information retrieval* (London, Deutsch 1965) gives descriptions with diagrams of some of the manual equipment. B C Vickery *On information retrieval (op cit)* provides a useful tabulation and diagrammatic representation of equipment related to systems on pages 137-138. C P Bourne's *Methods of information handling* (chapters five, six and nine) and J Becker and R M Hayes *Information storage and retrieval* (*op cit*) describe a wide range of equipment (including microform devices) and supply copious illustrations.

THE COMPUTER AND THE CATALOGUE
A closer relationship between information retrieval workers, with their varied array of mechanised systems, and cataloguers, with their relative lack of them, may be brought about by the increasing attention which both groups are paying to computers. Paradoxically enough, this is the most extensive piece of equipment in the field, but as more and more computer installations become available to the public and local authorities, to large business groups, to universities (many of them having a great deal of spare capacity), so it may become increasingly possible for the libraries associated with these various authorities to acquire some computer time for their own purposes.

A Opler 'An introduction to computers', pages 47-54 of W Simonton (ed) *Information retrieval today* (*op cit*) points out to librarians that, increasingly, computing will become a *service* function which is widely available. He points to the growth of the number of computers in the US (one in 1950, ten thousand twelve years later) and to the fact that, by use of telecommunication lines, it is perfectly possible to make use of a computer installation without being anywhere near it, or ever seeing the computer.

In the UK, which is much less computerised than the US, there has been nevertheless rapid development of interest in library automation in general and computerised cataloguing in particular, evidenced by the mounting number of reports, conferences, seminars and working parties.

In the proceedings of the Anglo-American conference on the mechanisation of library services held at Oxford, 1966, *Brasenose conference on the automation of libraries* edited by J Harrison and P Laslett (London, Mansell 1967), the balance of practical achievement favours the American delegation, which presents seven papers describing such developments as the LC automation programme, Project MARC, MEDLARS applications etc, while the three British papers amounted to little more than declarations of intent on the part of the British Museum, the Bodleian and Cambridge. In spite of the broader scope implied by its title, it is interesting to note that the conference largely concentrated on cataloguing operations. The Bodleian and other Oxford university libraries show up in a slightly better light in University of Oxford *Report of the committee on university libraries* (Oxford, 1966) in which chapter 4 pp 295-306 'Automation' deals in some detail with the prospect of a computerised cataloguing system and contains an explicit description of a system which might be employed. The report contains a specific recommendation bearing upon the provision of an automated book-form catalogue (p 200).

The Local and Public Authorities' computer panel *Computer applications in the library service: first report on cataloguing* (London, Local Government Computer Committee, 1967) presents the finding of a Libraries Working Party set up by the computer panel, and considers the problems of cataloguing in the light of the current expansion of published materials producing a national and international problem. Among its recommendations are: that BNB should be put in a position to catalogue all British publications (including government publications) and be given every facility for putting its current and past cataloguing data in machine-readable form; that current BNB output should be on magnetic tape available two or three weeks before the published lists; that SBN's should be carried in BNB and all other lists and references; that there should be a national union catalogue, or a network of union catalogues; that there should be a system developed for making use of the pre-1950 material (outside BNB's scope) contained in any computerised version of the BM *General catalogue*.

The proposal regarding current BNB output is in process of being achieved by means of a grant made by the Office of Scientific and Technical Information to BNB. As a result, a BNB 'MARC' project is now under way, comparable to the LC MARC project (*see* p 108), and catalogue data in the form of magnetic tape will be despatched weekly to participating libraries, the file containing a single sequence of entries in standard book number order with two printed indexes. The entries will carry a DC seventeenth edition number, a BNB classification number, a list of subject descriptors, added entries and references. The announcement of this development, 'Library network in MARC project' *Liaison* April 1968 (*inset* in *Library Association record* 70 (4) April 1968 21) further states that LC subject headings and class numbers will probably be added in due course, and since very close co-operation with the LC MARC project has been maintained, the two systems should be able to exchange data at an early stage.

A publication which covers recent developments in Britain is N S M Cox and M W Grose eds *Organization and handling of bibliographic records by computer* (Newcastle, Oriel Press 1967) which presents sixteen papers given at a four-day conference held at the University of Newcastle, 1967. The papers cover a wide range of matters, often reflecting work-in-progress or projects-in-hand, but all the same, producing more evidence of commitment than is indicated in the Brasenose conference proceedings. A comprehensive state-of-the-art report with an impressive bibliography is contained in an article by R T Kimber ' Computer applications in the fields of library housekeeping and information processing ' *Program: news of computers in British university libraries* (6) July 1967 5-25. (It might be noted that the above periodical has widened its scope to cover public and special libraries, from issue number 9 onwards being sub-titled ' news of computers in British libraries '.)

As a matter of record, public libraries have produced the first examples of computerised catalogues in Britain, without very much accompanying documentation. W R Maidment ' The computer catalogue in Camden ' *Library world* 67 (782) August 1965 40, gives an account of the book-form union catalogue produced, with updated author lists at fortnightly intervals and updated classified list with chain subject indexes at four-monthly intervals. Full cumulations, both author and classified, are supplied in bound volumes. This brief article sums up: ' The computer catalogue seems to be the only conceivable way of securing the advantages of a union catalogue in book form for a large system of libraries '. A C Meakin ' Production of a printed union catalogue by computer ' *Library Association record* 65 (9) September 1965 311-316 describes the system adopted in the London borough of Barnet, discussing advantages and disadvantages. Dorset County Library, using the county council's computer, issued a printed subject index in November 1965.

On the other side of the Atlantic, it has been mainly the large research and academic libraries which have tended to lead the way. E Heilinger 'Applications of advanced data processing techniques to university library procedures ' *Special libraries* 53 (8) October 1962 472-475 reported on work at Illinois. J M Perreault

The computerized book catalog at Florida Atlantic University' *College and research libraries* 25 (3) May 1964 185-197, R De-Gennaro 'A computer produced shelf list' [Harvard] *College and research libraries* 26 (4) July 1965 311-315, R Bregzis 'The Ontario new universities library project—an automated bibliographic data control system' *College and research libraries* 26 (6) November 1965 495-508, are all representative of the pattern of development, with the computerisation in some cases extending beyond the catalogue towards the automation of many related library procedures.

Useful summations of the American automation scene are provided in an article by H Bryan 'American automation in action' *Library journal* 92 (2) Jan 15 1967 189-196 and in the book by P Wasserman *The librarian and the machine* (Detroit, Gale 1965).

It has been, perhaps, the MEDLARS system (medical literature analysis and retrieval system) of the US National Library of Medicine which has exhibited so far the most dramatic demonstration of computer capabilities in both bibliographical control and indexing. Since August 1964 the monthly *Index medicus*, which analyses and indexes a vast proportion of the world's medical literature (the estimated amount for 1964 was about 175,000 monographs and periodical articles) has been produced by a large computer linked with a photo-composing machine fed by magnetic tape, which can set up copy in three founts of type. The system is also designed to yield current bibliographies in special areas of medicine, and special subject bibliographies (2,500 or more each year) on demand. It is envisaged that duplicate tapes of the stored index entries will eventually be made available to a number of large medical libraries throughout the world, a development of immense importance in medical documentation and indexing. A full description of the system is given by R F Garrard 'MEDLARS: systems engineering applied to libraries' pages 119-140 of W Simonton (ed) *Information retrieval today* (*op cit*). A useful evaluative comment is given by H Coblans in his chapter eleven 'Trends in research and development' pages 167-169 of R L Collison (ed) *Progress in library science 1965* (London, Butterworths 1965).

In the reference cited above Coblans also refers to what he calls ' the other great event in recent library history '—the Library of Congress proposals for automation—and summarises the background discussions and reports relating to complete automation that have been taking place for several years.

LC automation activities are based on the report by King G W and others *Automation and the Library of Congress* (Washington, LC 1963) which is concisely summarised by B E Markuson 'The United States Library of Congress automation survey' UNESCO *Bulletin for libraries* 19 (11) Jan-Feb 1965 24-34. The same writer has kept the picture up-dated with 'The Library of Congress automation program: a report to the stockholders' ALA *Bulletin* 61 (6) June 1967 647-655.

In 1966, the Library of Congress announced that one important part of the programme ' a project to test the feasibility of the central production and distribution of machine-readable catalogue data ' was under way and Project MARC (Machine Readable Catalog) came into being. Towards the end of 1966 it was distributing weekly tapes (each of which carried machine-readable data for about eight hundred titles) to the sixteen selected libraries participating in the experiment. The libraries receiving the magnetic tape processed it through their own computing facilities, the most common requirement being that of the production of catalogue cards. The pilot project was limited to cataloguing data for current English-language monographs and by the end of the test period, eight months after commencement, the complete tape carried some sixteen thousand entries. It is reported that a new format, MARC II, has been evolved as a result of the reports and recommendations of the participating libraries. It will meet the differing requirements of various libraries, with the emphasis on *convertibility* of the tapes rather than compatibility. Each library will be enabled, if it requires, easily to convert the data to its own desired format. to meet local conditions and its own catalogue features. One striking feature of automated cataloguing, already demonstrated in the swift transition from MARC I to MARC II, is the ability to make changes in procedures and practices that would not be feasible in a manual system. The Card Division of LC, beginning in the middle of 1968 will sell machine-readable records, to all interested libraries. P R Reimers ' The effective use of bibliographic information and the role of automation in the process ' *Libri* 17 (4) 1967 305-313 gives a very lucid account of Project MARC, its conclusions and its implications for the future. A briefer

statement appears in this same periodical issue in the section
'Automation (p 302) in the article by L Quincy Mumford
'Bibliographic developments at the Library of Congress' pp
294-304.

LC's role as a principal centre for the transmission of machine-readable data, taken in conjunction with its emergence as a global centre for the collection and transmission of catalogue data from similar centres in other countries through the Shared Cataloguing Programme, promises to open up an entirely new era for bibliographical control and cataloguing. The processes of automation do seem to offer endless possibilities for the improvement of library operations, and, inevitably, many further developments must take place.

On the one hand, there is speculation that the physical form of books and documents could be abandoned and their contents could be transferred to the vast memory of the computer, the bits being efficiently labelled for identification, indexed, and stored (*ie* catalogued), to be recalled, considered, compared, used, enriched, and re-filed by multiple users, each at his own console. Such is the kind of picture emerging from works by C F J Overhage ed *Intrex: report of a planning conference on information transfer experiments* (Cambridge, Mass, MIT Press 1965) and J C R Licklider *Libraries of the future* (Cambridge, Mass, MIT Press 1965).

On the other hand, presuming that the book and document as a physical form will persist for a long time ahead (and this is not an unreasonable assumption if only in respect of the sheer numbers of these items), there is yet the possibility that libraries will be seen as a network of document-centred communications storage systems, linked and operated by sophisticated computer methods which may make today's catalogues seem quite primitive instruments.

Whatever the future may bring, there can be little doubt but that any developments will owe much to the theory and practice of cataloguing, evolved by librarians for the systematic organisation of books, documents, and bibliographical records.

READINGS

W Ashworth *ed Handbook of special librarianship and information work* (London, ASLIB third edition 1967). Chapter thirteen, by the editor, 'A review of mechanical aids in library work' pages 524-553.

C D Needham *Organizing knowledge in libraries* (London, Deutsch 1964). Chapter twenty one 'Other retrieval devices'.

J R Sharp *Some fundamentals of information retrieval* (London, Deutsch 1965). 'The shortcomings of conventional systems', chapter four, are contrasted with 'The advantages of non-conventional systems', chapter five.

W Simonton *(ed) Information retrieval today* (Minneapolis, University of Minnesota, 1963). Papers (mostly by information retrieval specialists) presented at an institute conducted by the University of Minnesota library school. Nearly all the papers make useful reading for the purposes of the preceding chapter.

# SUBJECT INDEX

AA code *see* Anglo-American code, *1908*
AACR *see* Anglo-American cataloguing rules, *1967*
Academic libraries 94-95
Addressing machines 81
ALA Catalog Code Revision Committee 27, 31
ALA *Cataloguing rules, 1949* 27-29, 38-42
Alphabetico-classed catalogue 64
Alphabetico-specific catalogue 63
American Library Association *see* ALA
Analytical cataloguing 58, 90-91
*Anglo-American cataloguing rules, 1967* 11, 25, 32-37, 38-42, 84
*Anglo-American cataloguing rules, 1967*—nonbook materials 51-62
*Anglo-American code, 1908* 24-25, 38-42
Annotation 91-92
Anonymous works 38-39
ASLIB—Cranfield projects 101-102
Association of Research Libraries 32, 87
Author catalogues 17, 63
Author statement 46
Automation of cataloguing 12, 75, 104-109

Bibliographies and the catalogue 11, 91
Bibliothèque Nationale *Catalogue général* 17
Billings, John Shaw 19
Bodleian library 105
Book catalogue 74-75, 106
*Brasenose conference on the automation of libraries* 12, 45, 85, 104
*British catalogue of music* 54
British Museum catalogues 17, 75, 76, 82, 105
British Museum library 16
*British museum rules* 14-15, 21-22, 38-42
*British museum subject index* 19, 64
*British national bibliography* 16, 45, 67, 73, 82, 83-85, 93, 105-106
*British technology index* 71

Card catalogue 76-77
Card reproduction 80-82
Catalogue, function and purpose 9-12; inner form 63-73; physical form 74-78
Cataloguer's camera 82
Cataloguing, history of 14-20, 65-66
Cataloguing department—organisation 79-80
Cataloguing-in-source 86
Centralized cataloguing 82-88
Chain indexing 66-67
Chaplin, A H 30
Classification, faceted 100-101
Classified catalogue 18, 63, 64-68
*Code internationale de catalogage de la musique* 54
*Code of cataloguing rules* (Lubetzky) 30
Codes, comparisons between 38-49; development of 21-37; revision of 29-32
Collation statement 47
Compound surnames 41
Computer and the catalogue 12, 75, 93, 103, 104-109
Computer indexing—slides 62
Co-operative cataloguing 23
Co-ordinate indexing 98-100, 101
Corporate authorship 21, 24, 34, 35, 41-44
County libraries 93-94
Cranfield projects 101-102
Crestadoro, Andrea 15
CU—5 camera 82
Cutter, C A 15, 65
Cutter, C A *Rules for a dictionary catalog* 15, 22-23, 38-42, 65, 68-69

Descriptive cataloguing 34, 35, 44-48
Descriptive cataloguing—nonbook materials 51-62
Descriptors 99, 100
Dewey, Melvil 24, 66
Dictionary catalogue 18-19, 64, 65
Differences between British and American Texts, AACR 34-35
Different names, choice between 39-40

111

Divided catalogue 72
Duplication processes 80-82

Edge-notched cards 102
Editor statement 47
Electronic systems 102, 104-109
Entry, elements of 44-48

Faceted classification 100, 101
Films 51-52
Fortescue, G K 64

Gramophone records 55-56, 78
Guard-book catalogue 76

Haykin, D J 69, 72
History of cataloguing 14-20, 65

Illustrations and prints 60-62, 78
Imprint statement 47
Incunabula 59
*Index medicus* 107
Indexing, co-ordinate 98-100, 101
Indexing, subject 66-68
Information retrieval systems 97-103
Information retrieval systems—maps 57, 58
Information retrieval systems—slides 62
International Conference on Cataloguing Principles 10, 11, 30, 31, 36, 43
Item entry 99, 102

Jewett, Charles C 15
Joint authorship 38

Kaiser, J 70
Keyword-in-context (KWIC) index 100

Library Association Cataloguing Rules Subcommittee 27, 29, 31, 48
Library of Congress automation 73, 108-109
Library of Congress cards 83, 92
Library of Congress catalogues 17, 19, 35, 54, 56, 75, 82
Library of Congress *List of subject headings* 16, 69-70
Library of Congress *Rules for descriptive cataloguing* 16, 27-29
Librettos 53
Limited cataloguing 29, 89

Local and Public Authorities computer panel 105
London boroughs 93
*London Library catalogue* 17
*London Library subject index* 19
Lubetzky, S 11, 13, 30, 31, 43

Machine-readable catalogue data 85, 105, 108-109
Main entry 44-46; nonbook materials 50-62
Manual systems 102
Manuscripts 59
Maps 56-58
MARC project (BNB) 105-106
MARC project (LC) 108-109
Marginal punched cards 102
Mechanical systems 102
Medlars system 107
Microform devices—information retrieval 103
Microforms—cataloguing 58
Minicards 103
Mooers, C 98, 100
Municipal libraries 92-93
Music scores 52-55

NPAC *see* National program for acquisitions and cataloguing
Name catalogue 64
National program for acquisitions and cataloguing 86-88, 109
*National union catalog* 18, 75, 82
' No conflict ' policy 29
Nobility, titles of 40
Nonbook materials 50-62
Notes 48, 91

Offset lithography 81
Optical stencil cards 102
Oxford university libraries 105

Panizzi, Sir Anthony 14-15
Paris Conference *see* International Conference on Cataloguing Principles
Periodicals 35, 36, 39, 78, 97
Phonorecords 55-56
Photographs 60-62
Pictorial material 60-62
Prefixes to surnames 41
Printed card services 83-85, 92-95
Printed catalogue 74-75, 106

Project MARC (BNB) 105-106;—Project MARC (LC) 108-109
*Prussian instructions* 23-24, 43
Pseudonyms 40
Public libraries 92-94
Punched cards 103

Ranganathan, S R 66, 73, 86
Reactive catalogue 12
Relative index 66
Revision of cataloguing rules 29-32
Reproduction of catalogue entries 80-82
Rules, comparison of 38-49

SBN 84, 105
Sears *List of subject headings* 69-70
Selective cataloguing 89-90
Semantic code 101
Series statement 48
Shackleton *Report* 11, 105
Shared cataloguing 86-88, 109
Shaw, R R 103
Sheaf catalogue 77
Simplified cataloguing 88-90
Slides—cataloguing 62
Spalding, C S 31
Special libraries 95

Special materials 34, 50-62
Specific subject entry 22, 63, 68-70
Spirit duplicator 80
Standard book number 84, 105
Stencil duplicator 81
Subject catalogue 19-20; 63-64; 66-72
Subject cataloguing—nonbook materials 51-62
Surnames with prefixes 41

Term entry 99, 102
Title statement 46

Unit entry 45
Uniterms 98-99, 101
Universal Decimal Classification 101
University libraries 94-95
University of Oxford *Report of the Committee on University libraries* see Shackleton *Report*
Unknown authorship 38-39

*Vatican code* 25-27
Vickery, B C 100
Visible indexes 78

Wax-stencil duplicator 81

# INDEX OF AUTHORS CITED

The phrases in parentheses indicate the context in which the article or reading has been cited in the text, and do not represent exact title or subject. The full bibliographical details are given on the page indicated.

Allen, T E (Codes) 37
Ashmore, W S H (London borough catalogues) 93
Ashworth, W (Special libraries) 96; (Mechanical aids) 110

Bancroft, R (Catalogue forms) 64
Barnes, C (Records) 56
Becker, J. (Information retrieval) 101, 103
Bennett, F (London borough catalogues) 93
Benson, D (Simplified cataloguing) 90
Bourne, C P (Information retrieval) 100, 103
Bregzis, R (Purposes of cataloguing) 12; (Computer cataloguing) 107
Brockway, D (Microforms) 59
Brown, P (History) 17
Bryan, H (Automation) 107
Burkett, J (Maps) 57; (Microforms) 58; (Illustrations) 61, 62
Butcher, S J (Municipal libraries) 96

Chaplin, A H (Purposes of cataloguing) 11; (BM rules) 22; (Codes) 30, 31, 36
Cleverdon, C W (Cranfield project) 101
Coates, E J (Purposes of cataloguing) 12; (Chain indexing) 67; (Subject headings) 69, 71, 73
Coblans, H (Medlars) 107; (LC automation) 108
Costello, J C (Co-ordinate indexing) 100
Cowburn, L M (BNB use) 85
Cox, N S M (Computer cataloguing) 106

Crestadoro, A (History) 15
Crone, G R (Maps) 57
Cronin, J W (Shared cataloguing) 88
Cunningham, V (Music) 54
Custer, B A (Public libraries) 96
Cutter, C A (History) 15; (Purposes of cataloguing) 9-10; (Descriptive cataloguing) 48

Daily, J E (Special materials) 51
Davinson, D E (Visible indexes) 78
De Gennaro, R (Computer cataloguing) 107
Diatzko, K (Codes) 23
Dickman, D A (Codes) 37
Duncan, P S (Purposes of cataloguing) 11; (Codes) 28, 37; (Subject headings) 72

Easton, W E (Maps) 57
Eaton, T (Nonbook materials) 62
Egan, M (Classified catalogue) 68, 73
Englebarts, R K (Simplified cataloguing) 90
Field, F B (Codes) 36; (Limited cataloguing) 89
Fink, M E (Maps) 57
Francis, F C (BM rules) 22
Frarey, C J (Subject Headings) 72
Friedman, J (University libraries) 95
Fry, G (Card reproduction) 81

Garrard, R F (Medlars) 107
Gibbs-Smith, C H (Illustrations) 61
Goff, F R (Incunabula) 59
Gorman, M (Codes) 36
Grose, M W (Computer cataloguing) 106
Gull, C D (Catalogue forms) 78

Hagen, C B (Maps) 57
Hanson, J C M (Rules Comparison) 48
Harper, S F (BNB use) 85
Havard-Williams, P (Slides) 61
Hayes, R M (Catalogue forms) 75; (Information retrieval) 101, 103
Haykin, D J (Subject headings) 69
Heilinger, E (Computer cataloguing) 106
Henkle, H (Codes) 28
Hensel, E (Nonbook materials) 62
Hoare, P A (Codes) 31
Honoré, S (Corporate authorship) 44

Jackson, S L (Subject headings) 69
Jasenas, M (Manuscripts) 60
Jeffreys, A E (Main entry) 45; (University libraries) 95
Jewett, C C (History) 15
Jolley, L (Purposes of cataloguing) 12; (Codes) 29, 31; (Rules comparison) 49; (Catalogue forms) 64, 73; (Co-ordinate indexing) 100
Jones, G (County libraries) 94

Kaiser, J (Subject indexing) 70
Kieffer, P (Catalogue forms) 75
Kimber, R T (Computer applications) 106
King, G W (LC automation) 108
Kuvshinoff, B W (Slides) 61
Kyle, B R F (Special libraries) 95

Lewis, P R (Rules comparison) 49; (BNB use) 85, 93
Licklider, J C R (Library computerisation) 109
Linderfelt, K A (Codes) 23
Löhmann, O (Analytical cataloguing) 91
Lorenz, J G (Shared cataloguing) 88
Lubetzky, S (Purposes of cataloguing) 13; (History) 16; (Codes) 30; (Corporate authorship) 43
Luhn, H P (KWIC indexing) 100

McClellan, A W (Municipal libraries) 93
McDonald, M R (Catalogue forms) 75
McRee Elrod, J (Catalogue forms) 66

Maidment, W R (Computer cataloguing) 106
Mann, M (Purposes of cataloguing) 12; (Catalogue forms) 73, 78 (Cataloguing department) 96
Markuson, B E (LC automation) 108
Mason, D (Maps) 57; (Illustrations) 61; (Nonbook materials) 62
Meakin, A C (Computer cataloguing) 106
Metcalfe, J (History) 20; (Catalogue forms) 66; (Subject headings) 69, 73
Mills, J. (Chain indexing) 67
Mooers, C (Descriptors) 100
Morgan, T S (Maps) 57; (Microfilms) 58; (Illustrations) 61, 62
Mortimer, R S (University libraries) 96
Mumford, L Q (LC Project MARC) 109

Needham, C D (Codes) 23, 25, 37; (Rules comparison) 49; (Classified catalogue) 68; (Catalogue forms) 78; (Centralized cataloguing) 96; (Retrieval devices) 110
Norris, D M (History) 14; (Codes) 23; (Nonbook materials) 62; (Simplified cataloguing) 96

Olding, R K (Purposes of cataloguing) 12; (History) 15, 20; (Codes) 27; (Indexing) 71
Opler, A (Computers) 104
Osborn, A D (Codes) 24, 27, 29
Oustinoff, H (Cataloguer's camera) 82
Overhage, C F J (Project Intrex) 109

Palmer, B I (Chain indexing) 67
Pargeter, P S (Card reproduction) 81
Paulin, L (County libraries) 96
Perreault, J M (Computer cataloguing) 106
Pettee, J (History) 15, 20
Piggott, M (Purposes of cataloguing) 10; (Descriptive cataloguing) 48; (Catalogue forms) 78; (University libraries) 96

Ranganathan, S R (Rules comparison) 49; (Chain indexing) 66

Redfern, B (Music) 62
Reimers, P R (LC Project MARC) 108
Richmond, P A (Codes) 36
Richnell, D T (Microforms) 58
Robinson, C W (Catalogue forms) 75
Rogers, D (Illustrations) 61

Sharp, H A (History) 20; (Rules comparison) 49; (Catalogue forms) 66; (Annotation) 96
Sharp, J R (Special libraries) 96; (Information retrieval) 103; (Information retrieval systems) 110
Sharr, F A (Catalogue forms) 75
Shera, J H (Purposes of cataloguing) 10, 13; (Codes) 27, 29; (Classified catalogue) 68, 73; (Catalogue forms) 75
Simonton, W (Information retrieval) 100, 104, 110; (Medlars) 107
Skipper, J E (Shared catalogung) 88
Smith, E L J (Codes) 25
Somerville, S A (Records) 55
Spalding C S (Main entry) 45
Stranger, M H (Cataloguer's camera) 82
Strout, R F (History) 20
Swank, R C (Bibliographies) 91

Taube, M (Co-ordinate indexing) 98

Tauber, M F (Subject headings) 69; (Divided catalogue) 72; (Catalogue forms) 78
Tayler, A (History) 19
Taylor, R (Corporate authorship) 44
Treyz, J S (Card reproduction) 82
Trotier, A H (Cataloguing department) 96

Vasilevskaya, V A (Corporate authorship) 44
Vickery, B C (Semantic coding) 101; (Cranfield project) 101; (Information retrieval) 103
Viswanathan, C G (Codes) 24, 37

Walters, G (BNB use) 85
Ward, P (Annotation) 92
Wasserman, P (Library automation) 107
Watson, S A (Slides) 61
Welch, H M (Shared cataloguing) 88
Wells, A J (Main entry) 45; (Chain indexing) 67; (BNB cards) 83; (BNB) 85
Whitehouse, F (Card catalogues) 77
Williams, H D (Simplified cataloguing) 90
Williams, M (Cataloguer's camera) 82
Woods, B M (Maps) 57
Wright, J E (Visible indexes) 78